教育部人文社会科学研究青年基金项目
——西北回族聚居区需求响应式农村客运系统运力投放研究及行车路径鲁棒优化研究（项目批准号：18YJC630118）成果

农村需求响应式客运系统运力投放研究及行车路径鲁棒优化

Capacity Allocation and Route Robust Optimization of the Demand-responsive Rural Passenger Transport System

——Taking Linxia Hui Autonomous Prefecture as an Example

——以临夏回族自治州为例

马昌喜　赵永鹏　王　超　焦俞端 ◎ 著

西南交通大学出版社
·成　都·

图书在版编目（ＣＩＰ）数据

农村需求响应式客运系统运力投放研究及行车路径鲁棒优化: 以临夏回族自治州为例 = Capacity Allocation and Route Robust Optimization of the Demand-responsive Rural Passenger Transport System—— Taking Linxia Hui Autonomous Prefecture as an Example : 英文/ 马昌喜等著. —成都: 西南交通大学出版社，2022.5

ISBN 978-7-5643-8422-7

Ⅰ. ①农… Ⅱ. ①马… Ⅲ. ①农村 – 公路运输 – 旅客运输 – 行车组织 – 研究 – 临夏回族自治州 – 英文 Ⅳ. ①U492.2

中国版本图书馆 CIP 数据核字（2021）第 254355 号

农村需求响应式客运系统运力投放研究及行车路径鲁棒优化
——以临夏回族自治州为例

马昌喜　赵永鹏　王　超　焦俞端　著

责 任 编 辑	张文越
封 面 设 计	何东琳设计工作室
出 版 发 行	西南交通大学出版社 （四川省成都市金牛区二环路北一段 111 号 西南交通大学创新大厦 21 楼）
发行部电话	028-87600564　028-87600533
邮 政 编 码	610031
网 　 址	http://www.xnjdcbs.com
印 　 刷	四川煤田地质制图印刷厂
成 品 尺 寸	148 mm × 210 mm
印 　 张	6.875
字 　 数	208 千
版 　 次	2022 年 5 月第 1 版
印 　 次	2022 年 5 月第 1 次
书 　 号	ISBN 978-7-5643-8422-7
定 　 价	35.00 元

Since the reform and opening up, road passenger transport industry in China has been developed rapidly, which greatly facilitates the people travelling, and powerfully promotes economic and cultural exchanges and cooperation, as well as providing a good transportation atmosphere for the national economy and social development. However, at the same time, we should also be aware that there are still many contradictions and problems in rural passenger transport.

Cultivating and developing rural passenger transport is of great significance for improving the structural adjustment of the road transport industry and achieving great-leap-forward development. In recent years, with rapid development of China's national economic construction, the development of rural passenger transport market is becoming more and more prosperous. However, due to the peculiarities of rural passenger transport and the natural geography of rural areas, coupled with a series of reasons, such as the backwardness of rural road infrastructure, the variety of operating vehicles and vehicle models, the lack of scientific transport organization and management, etc., the rural passenger transport market reveals a low utilization rate of vehicles, high empty driving rate, unsaturated passenger sources, and large difference between "hot and cold" lines, thus leading to the "scattered, chaotic, mixed, small" performance phenomenon, and low security. Therefore, how to speed up the construction of rural roads and improve the level of passenger transport on rural roads is a urgently required topic.

This book will attempt to solve the problems above and contribute to the revitalization of rural areas and the transportation power strategy.

In the process of writing, the book references a great deal of literatures. We would like to express our high respect and heartfelt thanks to the authors of the literature.

For this book, many thanks go to my students, Lu Xijin, Chen Siyuan, Wang Ke, Zhao Minghui, Guo Jin, Wu Yuankun, Yang Yun and Jiao Yuduan, for their proofreading support.

We would like to particularly acknowledge the Ministry of Education in China because this research is funded by the Program of Humanities and Social Science of Education Ministry of China under Grant No. 18YJC630118. This work was also supported by the "Double-First Class" Major Research Programs, Educational Department of Gansu Province (No. GSSYLXM-04), and the Foundation of A Hundred Youth Talents Training Program of Lanzhou Jiaotong University.

Ma Changxi, Zhao Yongpeng, Wang Chao, Jiao Yuduan
School of Traffic and Transportation, Lanzhou Jiaotong University
Oct. 1, 2021

Chapter 1

Overview

1.1 Introduction

The Hui nationality is the most widely distributed ethnic group in China. According to the statistics of the seventh national census, the total population of Hui is about 9, 816, 800. Most of the population gather in northwest China, such as Ningxia, Gansu, Qinghai and Xinjiang. There are unique natural landscapes and humanities, as well as huge development potential, market capacity and development prospects here. However, due to the constraints of various factors such as natural, economic and historical development, it is difficult and inconvenient for farmers to travel.

From the beginning time of reform and opening-up, the road passenger demand has developed rapidly. At the same time, we should also be sober to recognize that there are still many contradictions and problems in rural passenger transport. It is mainly based on the following four aspects. The first is that the company is small, the market is not strong, and the ability to resist risks is poor. The second is that the market is low, the quality of employees is generally not high, and the quality of service is difficult to meet the increasing requirements for people. The third is the lack of safe protection. Major and catastrophic accidents occur from time to time, and the safety of lives and property for people cannot be safeguarded. The forth is low service levels which is difficult to adapt to the needs of the broad masses of the people. Compared with the city passenger transport, the rural passenger transport has many points, long lines, wide surface, low ticket price, unstable passenger flow, and is obviously limited by road conditions and vehicle conditions.

Cultivating and developing rural passenger transport are important for improving the structure adjustment of road transportation industry and achieving leap-forward development. In recent years, with the acceleration of national economic construction of our country, the development of rural passenger transportation is more flourishing. However, rural passenger transport and rural natural geographical conditions have particularity. There are many kinds of rural road infrastructure, many types of operating vehicles, and lacking of scientific transportation organization and management model. As a result, there is a phenomenon that the rural passenger transport market is low, the empty drive rate is high, and it has high passenger and unsaturated, the wire is high, and the overall presence is "scattered, chaotic, miscellaneous, small", also, the safety is low. There are some problems in the rural passenger market, such as: the vehicle utilization rate is low, the empty drive rate is high, the number of customers is not saturated, and the degree of crowding of the line is different. These overall presented a phenomenon of "scattered, chaotic, miscellaneous, small" which makes low security of the rural passenger market. Therefore, how to speed up the construction of rural roads, enhance rural road passenger transport level, and realize rural rejuvenation is a topic that needs to be studied.

1.2 Literature review

1.2.1 Research status of passenger transportation capability

Capacity delivery is the key content of the optimal allocation for rural passenger transport resources. In a broad sense, transport capacity refers to the comprehensive forces of people, finance, property and management directly related to transportation. The capacity of rural passenger transport refers to the actual direct passenger transport capacity of a vehicle specializing in rural passenger transport on a rural road. Rural passenger transport capacity includes two parts: one is to determine the capacity delivery quota. The other is to determine the capacity delivery mode, i.e., the allocation of transport capacity.

Due to the diverse social and economic backgrounds, different perfection of transportation infrastructure and different coverage of rural passenger transport, the research and research achievements of rural passenger transport are not identical.

In the 1980s, due to wide and sparsely populated, the number of cars per capita was high in European and American countries. European and American national passenger transport companies had withdrawn from rural areas due to their very low returns. According to statistics, nearly 40 percent of rural areas in the United States had no public transport services in 2002, and 28 percent had very few public transport services[1]. At this time, academia began to study the related transport theory. They advocated providing convenient, flexible and efficient public transportation for rural areas to serve vulnerable groups such as the elderly and the disabled living. Since then, foreign countries began to research the rural passenger transport system. However, the research direction focused on policy improvement[2-3], government subsidies[4-5] and rural passenger service operation[6-7]. In terms of capacity delivery in rural passenger transport system, Taofiki[8] and Sabina[9] studied the impact of car ownership and gender on rural passenger transport demand respectively.

With the construction of a new socialist countryside in China, improving the travel conditions of farmers has become a top priority. After 2004, our rural passenger transport planning and its research began to get wide attention. In terms of transport capacity allocation, in view of the network structure of rural passenger transport market and the travel characteristics of rural residents, Feng used non-aggregate theory to study the travel characteristics of rural population, constructed a multi-target, also, constrained and non-linear transport capacity structure distribution model[10]. Hu put forward the dry and branch planning method and the method of estimline capacity allocation using the maximum section flow estimation method at peak hour according to the road network structure of rural passenger transport market and residents' travel characteristics[11]. Li studied the allocation scale and structure of rural passenger transport in the western mountainous area, and established the capacity scale allocation scheduling model and regional capacity optimization method with regional operation as the main body[12]. Luo used the gray forecast model and the non-aggregate MNL forecast model to predict the rural passenger volume and residents' travel mode respectively, and put forward the calculation formula of the main trunk distribution and the branch distribution strategy[13]. By analyzing the spatial and temporal characteristics of rural passenger flow, Liu predicted the volume of rural passenger flow, and analyzed the rationality of this method with practical data[14]. Wu and Liu elaborated on the factors affecting the release of rural passenger transport capacity, put forward the new concept of the minimum daily operation shift, and constructed the calculation formula[15]. Guo put forward the decision model of road transport capacity control by studying the influencing factors of highway passenger transport demand and regulating passenger transport capacity[16]. Hu and Tang believed that the study of rural passenger transport capacity allocation should start from the two aspects of transport capacity scale allocation and transport capacity structure allocation, and analyzed the internal and external factors affecting the allocation of rural passenger transport capacity[17]. Wei established and contrasting analyzed the departure interval model of three rural passenger lines, and then determined the number of lines[18].

The existing researches on the transport capacity release of rural passenger transport system are more inclined to qualitative analysis[19-21] and policy interpretation[22-23], which lacks a degree of rigor, and cannot provide powerful help for the optimization of rural passenger transport resources. Therefore, the construction of a reasonable and accurate rural passenger transport system transport capacity delivery model is the most important task of rural passenger transport system research.

1.2.2 Research status of the demand-responsive rural passenger transport system

The characteristics of rural areas are low road grade, low road density and relatively scattered village layout. Therefore, the rural passenger transport problem cannot directly apply the urban passenger transport planning. Back in the 1960s, western cities began to expand into low-density areas. In 1968, Cole proposed a mode of travel to solve travel problems in low-density areas based on the Dial-a-Bus model. This was considered to be the prototype of demand-responsive buses[24]. In 1984, Daganzo pioneered the basic concept of demand responsive buses and proved that demand responsive buses performed better in low travel density areas than regular bus services[25]. In 1999, Malucelli proposed the Demand adaptive systems (DAS)[26], which has been studied more extensively and deeply by scholars including Crainic[27] and Malucelli[28]. Since then, the demand-responsive bus and the demand-adapted passenger service system have been paid attention to by experts and scholars, and the organization mode of rural passenger transport system is mostly based on both. Corine Mully pointed that the model can be used as an important model for rural passenger transport recovery due to the flexibility of the demand-responsive systems[29]. Xu summed up the experience and lessons of foreign applied demand-responsive passenger transport system, and analyzed its adaptability, also, he used the method of applicable scenario simulation to simulate the line planning and fare design of the demand-responsive systems in rural areas. However, the case framework selected was quite different from the actual situation in rural areas in China, which cannot truly reflect the performance of the Demand adaptive systems in the passenger transport system in rural areas[30]. Zohora et al. integrated the flexible passenger system sample data in the rural area of Texas. A set of measurement economics is then proposed to provide reference and basis for the size decision of the government's flexible passenger transport system in rural areas[31]. Some scholars had tried to use the demand-responsive systems to combine rural passenger transport and express delivery to improve transport efficiency, this will increase the profits of rural passenger transport companies by addressing the problem of express delivery[33].

At present, there is still little research on the driving path optimization of the passenger transport system in rural areas. A related model and empirical study have been established for the online layout and line planning of flexible operational mode, and the cases, including Dandapat[34] and Lima[35], etc. Zhang et al, optimized the line plan according to the rural area passenger demand, and calculated the radiode mode, the regional line mode, and the cyclic line mode[36].

According to the characteristics of rural areas of our courtry, Zhang Qiang integrated the advantages of demand response bus and demand adaptive passenger service system to design a new rural passenger service system and path optimize it[37].

1.2.3 Literature analysis

To sum up, most of the existing research results of rural passenger transport system focus on operation organization, station layout and station layout, and few literature focuses on the study of rural passenger transport capacity allocation and vehicle path optimization of rural passenger transport system. Moreover, most of the existing literature studies the resource allocation problem of rural passenger transport system from the perspective of economics, and less implements it to the specific vehicle path optimization. Therefore, the study of rural passenger transport system capacity delivery and robust vehicle path optimization can proceed from the needs of rural passenger transport. And it can settle on the specific implementation of the organizational form of the demand-responsive rural passenger transport system, guide the rural passenger transport to the direction in which the service is more efficient and the operating cost is lower and solve the problem of difficulty in travel in rural residents, which makes practical contributions to rural areas, and has strong practical significance.

1.3 Summary

This chapter first analyzes the research background of the demand responsive rural passenger transport system. Then, the research status of passenger transportation capability and the demand-responsive passenger transport system are reviewed respectively.

1.4 References

[1] Stommes E S, Brown D M. Moving rural residents to work: lessons from eight job access and reverse commute projects[J]. Transportation Research Record, 2005, 1903(1): 44-53.

[2] Mackie, Peter. The UK transport policy white paper[J]. Journal of Transport Economics and Policy, 1998, 32(3): 399–403.

[3] Gordon C A. Planning for an unpredictable future: transport in Great Britain in 2030[J]. Transport Policy, 2006, 13(3): 254-264.

[4] Hensher D A, Wallis I P. Competitive tendering as a contracting mechanism for subsidising transportation: the bus experience[J]. Journal of Transport Economics and Policy, 2005(39): 1-25.

[5] Pucher J, Kurth S. Verkehrsverbund: the success of regional public transport in Germany, Austria and Switzerland[J]. Transport Policy, 1995, 2(4): 279-291.

[6] Velaga N R, Nelson J D, Wright S D, et al. The potential role of flexible transport services in enhancing rural public transport provision[J]. Journal of Public Transportation, 2012, 15(1): 111-131.

[7] Kumarage A S, Weerawardena J, Piyasekera R. A concession model to promote rural bus services in Sri Lanka[P]. Conference on Competition and Ownership Inland Passenger Transport, 2009, 1-18.

[8]　Salau T. Public transportation in metropolitan Lagos, Nigeria: analysis of public transport users' socioeconomic characteristics[J]. Urban Planning & Transport Research, 2015, 3(1): 132-139.

[9]　Mahapa S, Mashiri M. Social exclusion and rural transport: gender aspects of a road improvement project in Tshitwe, Northern Province[J]. Development Southern Africa, 2001, 18(3): 365-376.

[10]　Zhongxiang Feng. Study on the rural population travel characteristics and the distribution model of transport capacity structure[D]. Xi'an: Chang 'an University, 2010.

[11]　Kunpeng Hu. Study on the application of county rural passenger transport planning method[D]. Guangzhou: South China University of Technology, 2014.

[12]　Bo Li. Research on western mountainous rural passenger capacity configuration[D]. Chongqing: Chongqing Jiaotong University, 2013.

[13]　Wei Luo. Analysis of rural passenger transport in Chongqing[D]. Chongqing: Chongqing Jiaotong University, 2011.

[14]　Yali Liu. Research on the development planning of rural passenger transport system[D]. Xi'an: Chang'an University, 2013.

[15]　Qiang Wu, Xu Liu. Research on the delivery strategy of rural passenger transport capacity[J]. Transportation and Transportation (Academic Edition), 2008(1): 70-72.

[16]　Wei Guo. Study on decision-making referring model of road passenger transport capacity regulation[J]. Urban Roads Bridges & Flood Control, 2011, 9(9)：245-247.

[17] Shaofeng Hu, Huajiao Tang. Analysis of influencing factor of rural passenger transportation capacity configuration[J]. Traffic Standardization, 2010(2): 111-113.

[18] Lin Wei. Research on rural passenger transport capacity allocation and operation management based on urban-rural integration[D]. Nanjing: Southeastern University, 2013.

[19] Fang Huang. Development strategy of rural passenger transport in Chongqing based on SWOT analysis[J]. Transportation Technology and Economy, 2021, 23(2): 68-74.

[20] Yang Yuan. Study on capacity model of rural passenger network[J]. Scientific and Technological Innovation, 2017(26): 24-25.

[21] Bo Li, Jinshan Chen. Research on passenger capacity scheduling in China's west mountainous rural areas[J]. Road traffic and safety, 2014, 14(5): 56-60.

[22] Xing Lei, Mei Zhong. Current situation and analysis of rural passenger transport development in Sichuan province[J]. Transport Energy Conservation and Environmental Protection, 2019, 15(3): 27-30.

[23] Bingqian Xiu, Xuling Fang. Analysis of the current situation and countermeasures of rural passenger transport in western mountainous areas[J]. Transportation Enterprise Management, 2015, 30(8): 10-12.

[24] Cole L, Merritt H. Tomorrow's transportation : new systems for the urban future[M]. U.S. Government Printing Office, 1968.

[25] CF Daganzo. Checkpoint dial-a-ride systems[J]. Transportation Research Part B, 1984, 18(4/5): 315-327.

[26]   Malucelli F, Nonato M, Pallottino S. Demand adaptive systems: some proposals on flexible transit 1[M]. Palgrave Macmillan UK, 1999.

[27]   Crainic T G, Malucelli F, Nonato M, et al. Meta-Heuristics for a class of demand-responsive transit systems[J]. Informs Journal on Computing, 2005, 17(1): 10-24.

[28]   Malucelli F, Nonato M, Crainic T G. Adaptive memory programming for a class of demand responsive transit systems. Computer-Aided Scheduling of Public Transport, 2001(505): 253-273.

[29]   Corinne Mulley a, John D. Nelson b. Flexible transport services: A new market opportunity for public transport[J]. Research in Transportation Economics, 2009, 25(1): 39-45.

[30]   Rongrong Xu. Research of DRT application in rural passenger transport[D]. Xi'an: Chang'an University, 2015.

[31]   Sultana Z, Mishra S, Cherry C R, et al. Modeling frequency of rural demand response transit trips[J]. Transportation Research Part A, 2018(118): 494-505.

[32]   Fatnassi E, Chaouachi J, Klibi W. Planning and operating a shared goods and passengers on-demand rapid transit system for sustainable city-logistics[J]. Transportation Research Part B, 2015(81): 440-460.

[33]   Yan Gao. Route Design of village-town passenger transport operating express delivery[D]. Beijing: Beijing Jiaotong University, 2020.

[34] Dandapat S, Maitra D. An approach for identifying optimal service for rural bus routes[J]. Case Studies on Transport Policy, 2015, 3(3): 287-294.

[35] Souza Lima F M, Pereira D S, Conceicao S V, et al. A mixed load capacitated rural school bus routing problem with heterogeneous fleet: Algorithms for the Brazilian context[J]. Expert Systems with Applications, 2016, 56(9): 320-334.

[36] Fengyan Zhang., Wei Zhou. Optimization of rural bus route based on traffic compactness[J]. Journal of Highway and Transportation Research and Development, 2010 (9): 112-116.

[37] Qiang Zhang, Qi Yang. Research on integrated rural passenger service model based on mobile passenger service[J]. Journal of Highway and Transportation Research and Development, 2014 (7): 332-336.

Chapter 2

Development trend of rural passenger transport

2.1 Related concepts

2.1.1 Rural highway

Unlike urban areas, rural highway is a road that serves rural production and life as well as agricultural economic development and meets certain technical standards, in addition to national and provincial highway. The rural highway referred to in this book serve the travel needs of the majority of farmers and mainly connect rural traffic distribution points such as counties, towns and villages. It generally includes three levels of county road, township road and village road, but excludes tractor road and field road [1].

Table 2.1 Classification of rural highway in China

No.	Classification		Application
1	Rural highway	External Contact	Connecting rural economic organizations and their regional business centers
2		Internal Contact	Connecting production units at all levels within rural economic organizations and enterprise business centers
3	Tractor road		Connects production units at all levels of operation centers and field blocks
4	Field road		Meet the needs of farmers for field management

In April 2007, the situation of rural highway of different administrative levels and different technical levels in the east, central and west of China is shown in Table 2.2 below. The eastern region of China includes 11 provinces (cities), Beijing, Tianjin, Hebei, Liaoning, Shanghai, Jiangsu, Zhejiang, Fujian, Shandong, Guangdong and Hainan. The central region includes 8 provinces (regions), Shanxi, Jilin, Heilongjiang, Anhui, Jiangxi, Henan, Hubei and Hunan. The western region includes 12 provinces (cities), Sichuan, Chongqing, Guizhou, Yunnan, Tibet, Shaanxi, Gansu, Qinghai, Ningxia, Xinjiang, Guangxi and Inner Mongolia.

Table 2.2 The proportion of rural highway of different administrative levels in each region of China

Partition	County road	Township road	Accomodation highway	Village road
National	17.12%	33.32%	1.68%	47.89%
Eastern	13.83%	34.91%	1.17%	50.10%
Central	13.69%	30.64%	0.85%	54.82%
Western	23.27%	34.65%	2.92%	39.17%

As can be seen from Table 2.2, in terms of county road, the west is higher than the east and central. In terms of township road, there is not much difference between the east, central and west. And in terms of village road, the east and central are much higher than the west. It shows that there is still a lot of room for improvement in rural highway in the western region, and improving rural highway is the basis and prerequisite for achieving good development of rural passenger transport.

2.1.2 Rural passenger transport

In a broad sense, rural passenger transport [2] is a passenger transport service that includes a variety of means of transportation, such as shuttle passenger transport, cabs, private cars, tricycles, motorcycles, passenger-carrying agricultural vehicles, ferries, etc., to provide transportation services for residents traveling in rural areas. Statistics show that the proportion of highway passenger transportation is 90%. In various modes of transport, short-and medium-distance rural passenger transport is a very important part, which has obvious competitive advantages. The rural passenger transport referred to in this book is the production activity within the county or with neighboring counties, where at least one end of the operating route [3] is in the rural areas, with the highway as the operating base, the passenger vehicle as the means of transportation, and the rural passenger transport station as the operation base for the purpose of passenger displacement. Among them, rural passenger transport routes refer to the shuttle bus operation paths within the county or between neighboring counties with at least one end of the operation line in rural areas, including the route types from the county to the township village, township to township, township to village, etc.

2.1.3 Rural passenger flow

In terms of the ontogeny of travel, passenger demand is derived from the ontogenetic demand of socio-economic activities, and the rural passenger demands is no exception. Rural passenger traffic is the sum of travel with a fixed direction formed by the traveler in order to achieve a certain travel purpose. The main body of travel is the vast number of rural people, travel mode includs class line passenger transport, cabs, private cars, tricycles, motorcycles, passenger-carrying agricultural vehicles, ferries. There are several characteristics of rural passenger flow as follows.

1. Single travel purpose and simple travel structure

The purpose of rural residents' travel is relatively single. According to the survey of 1, 782 questionnaires of rural residents, rural residents' travel is generally divided into going out to work during agricultural leisure, visiting friends and relatives during festivals, shopping and going out to do business. Among them, the proportion of shopping is the largest, 41%. And the influence of different genders and ages on the composition of residents' travel purpose is also different. Due to the difference in social division of labor and the difference in physical and psychological strength between men and women, the demand for rural passenger transport is different. Young and middle-aged males predominate in going out to work, and middle-aged females predominate in visiting relatives and friends. The survey of rural residents' travel purpose is shown in Table 2.3[4].

Table 2.3   Survey on travel purpose of rural residents

Travel purpose	Outworking	Visiting friends and relatives	Shopping	Going to work or school	Outbound	Others	Total
number of people	112	342	730	315	274	9	1782
proportion	6.3%	19.2%	41%	17.7%	15.3%	0.5%	100%

2. Uneven passenger flow and scattered passenger sources

Rural passenger transport shows a certain unevenness in time and space. In space, residents live in clusters of villages, houses are scattered and not concentrated, and the mobile population is small, making the difference between different lines is huge. Some lines have long distances, through the densely populated areas, the passenger source is sufficient. Other lines through remote villages and populated mountainous areas, the empty seat rate is relatively high, and cannot even maintain normal operating costs. In time, the rural highway passenger travel time is more concentrated, mostly for the market or out of work. In particular, the market is crowded with a serious shortage of vehicles, but the market is not a surplus of vehicles, the passenger source is unstable, with outstanding time and unidirectional.

3. Lack of organized operation and low utilization rate of vehicles

Due to the lack of organized operation, the main operators are mostly individual, small-scale, low degree of intensification, showing diversity, scattered, weak posture and other characteristics. Practitioners of their own quality varies, the level of business services is low, business conflicts are more prominent, resulting in long-term downturn in rural passenger transport, simply cannot be compared with any urban bus lines. At the same time, due to the economy and the own characteristics of the rural passenger flow, rural passengers mostly leave early and return late form, which makes the rural residents transport mostly short-distance transport, and subject to seasonal influences. The volatility of rural passenger flow is greater, it is difficult to achieve the fixed point, fixed class, fixed line operation, the vehicle utilization rate is low.

2.1.4 Demand-responsive rural transit

Reservation responsive rural bus is through the phone or network APP, to provide charter, carpool passenger transport services. It is the underwriting solution to the demand for safe and convenient travel for the masses in remote areas, low passenger flow, and the inability to meet the demand of ordinary operation methods (shuttle passenger transport, bus passenger transport). Demand-responsive rural bus is a reservation-based travel service that requires a reservation application 24 hours in advance. After the rural bus control center or bus company receives the reservation application, it needs to process it and feedback the results to passengers by phone or cell phone app, so that passengers can better prepare for their trips and make reasonable arrangements to complete their trips successfully.

2.1.5 Rural residents travel

The term "travel" had been defined differently at different times and in different books, and travel was defined in Traffic Engineering as the movement of people, materials or cars from one place to another [5]. In this case, the movement of a person is called a personal trip. Some people define travel as the whole process of movement of people, vehicles and goods from the point of departure to the destination, which are called residential travel, vehicle travel and goods travel, respectively[6]. All of the above are defined in terms of the action process completed by the subject of travel, i.e., the subject and the result of travel are described, but the motive, purpose, and mode of travel are not given a clear expression.

In transportation planning, the number of urban residents' travels is often counted in terms of neighborhoods, i.e., a travel beyond a certain block area is a travel. Due to the complexity of urban residents' travel activities, it is easy to move from one neighborhood to another or more neighborhoods, and a one-way travel is a travel, so urban residents often include many travels in one "outing". Unlike urban residents, rural residents' travels have a wider range of activities, less variation in travel, and a single purpose of travel, often to towns. In addition, rural residents work closer to their homes, often within the coverage of the village, the distance is short, and the number of daily work is high, so the activities carried out due to daily work cannot be classified as travel.

Therefore, for rural residents' travel, this paper defines it as the process of rural residents starting from villages, transported by vehicles, and reaching their destinations.

2.1.6 Travel demand

Travel demand, which can also be referred to as transportation demand, refers to people's need to travel in time and space in order to carry out activities such as social production and daily life. The activity analysis approach, on the other hand, considers travel demand as a need derived from people's need to satisfy their personal or family needs and to participate in activities held on spatially distant sites, rather than just to travel [7].

Activity refers to the process by which an individual uses a certain mode of arrival and priority to achieve a certain purpose at a certain location within a continuous period of time. Activities corresponding to travel can be classified as work activities, recreational activities, etc. Since each person has to arrange activities according to his or her own will, travel is required in order to connect the various activities that differ in time and space [8]. Thus, it is clear that activity is the most fundamental, which triggers travel and also influences travel elements such as destination and time. Therefore, activity-based travel theory argues for predicting travel demand based on activity, and its basic ideas can be summarized in the following four points.

(1) The demand for human travel stems from the need for socio-economic activities.

(2) In the process of travel, human behavior is limited by time and space to carry out different activities at different times and places and go to each activity location with time and space changes.

(3) Families influence individuals' activity and travel decisions. Many decisions are made as part of family decisions and are limited by

other members of the family as well as by the specific circumstances of the family. So both family type and lifestyle will influence individual choices.

(4) Human activity and travel decisions are dynamic and decisions are influenced by past and anticipated events.

2.2   The current situation of rural passenger transport development

As the main mode of travel for rural residents, rural passenger transport undertakes the main passenger transportation between urban and rural areas and plays an increasingly prominent role in promoting the process of integrated development of rural and urban areas. Rural passenger transport mainly refers to passenger transport from county and city to township, between townships, township to village and between villages. The proportion of our population distributed in rural areas is large, and it is an important part of the highway passenger transport system. Rural passenger transport connects counties, cities and surrounding rural areas, which can improve the depth of vertical coverage of highway passenger transport network, facilitate the travel of rural residents and meet the personal interests of urban and rural residents.

1. The process of rural passenger transportation network faster

In recent years, governments at all levels have been increasing the financial investment and policy support for rural passenger transport. Especially with the continuous construction of rural highway. By the end of 2020, the total number of rural passenger stations were 330, 000, and the total number of rural passenger vehicles were 320, 000.

2. Passenger yard is gradually built and improved

In accordance with the construction requirements of synchronous planning, synchronous design, synchronous construction and synchronous acceptance with the construction of rural highway, by 2005, the average rate of construction of township-level passenger transport stations was 22% in China, 41% in the east, 23% in the center and 14% in the west. Rural passenger transport infrastructure has been improved as never before, and the travel conditions of rural residents and waiting conditions have been greatly improved.

3. Gradual optimization of vehicle structure

In view of the actual situation of many old passenger vehicles and poor safety performance in rural areas, effective measures have been taken to encourage operators to update their vehicles and significantly upgrade the capacity structure. By the end of 2010, the national rural passenger transport vehicles reached 380, 000. Zhejiang, Chongqing and other regions actively promoted economic, safe and applicable "rural bus", greatly improving the travel conditions of rural residents and providing a guarantee for transport safety.

4. Passenger transport organization and management level improvement

In order to change the main body of rural passenger transport does not adapt to the current situation of transport needs, the competent transport departments around the adjustment of the main structure of the business to start, and actively guide the rural passenger transport operators to corporatization or joint operation. Unified site, unified scheduling, unified fares, unified vehicle identification and unified settlement to improve efficiency, standardize behavior and improve the purpose of service. Such as Zhejiang Province, the transport department by encouraging rural passenger transport operators to take shareholding system transformation, area operation, professional management and other ways to accelerate the pace of intensive operation, and promote the healthy development of rural passenger transport.

5. Passenger transport market order improvement

Township transport management stations and other departments to deepen the rural passenger transport market, strengthen market supervision and improve the depth of industry management. Focus on solving the prevalence of rural passenger transport market rip-offs and other outstanding issues, through the elimination of old passenger vehicles, to improve the safety awareness of drivers and passengers and other measures to crack down on tractors, agricultural transport vehicles, motor tricycles and other illegal operations. The travel safety of the peasants has been strongly protected, the passenger transport market order has improved significantly, and the legitimate rights and interests of the peasants have been effectively safeguarded.

2.3 Problems in the development of rural passenger transport

The rapid development of rural passenger transport has created better travel conditions for the rural masses and promoted rural economic and social development and progress. However, due to various factors, the development of rural passenger transport is greatly constrained and faces many problems, which are highlighted by the following points.

(1) The level of development is low. Some highways are not open to traffic, the frequency of traffic is low and other problems exist in large numbers, the rural masses, especially in remote mountainous areas, the problem of difficult access to transport has not been fundamentally solved.

(2) Policy support is not enough. Rural passenger transport public welfare characteristics are extremely obvious, objectively require the government to support from the policy and the financial subsidies, in the past there was a lack of supporting policies and measures to support subsidies.

(3) Insufficient management methods. The existing rural passenger transport business model is single, the vehicle equipment level is low, the management base and strength are weak, the management means and methods are relatively backward, safety supervision is difficult.

The main factors affecting and limiting the development of rural passenger transport are as follows [9].

(1) Poor highway condition. The technical level of rural highway is relatively low, a considerable part of the rainfall and other factors cannot be normal traffic, maintenance management is not enough, "back to the rotten rate" is high, the lack of safety infrastructure, it is difficult to meet the requirements of safe passage of vehicles, and

access to the depth is not enough, rural highway network to be formed.

(2) The construction of passenger transport stations lags behind. Rural passenger transport with highway, vehicles, no station phenomenon prevails. Some towns and villages do not have grade passenger stations, and more than 90% of administrative villages with passenger vehicles do not have request stop. Most rural passenger vehicles are basically in the backward state of roadside departure, open-air waiting, the majority of rural people in the "sunny day covered with ash, rainy day covered with mud" in the poor riding environment.

(3) Weak safety foundation. Rural passenger transport is widely distributed, scattered operations and lack of sites, which is at the edge of the management scope. The coordination mechanism between the relevant departments is not complete, the safety management force and the foundation is relatively weak.

(4) Market order is chaotic. Rural passenger transport market does not operate in accordance with the approved areas, lines, transferring and reversing passengers, string line operation and other irregularities prevail, a large number of motorcycles, tricycles, Chang'an cars, agricultural vehicles, scrap cars and other illegal social vehicles flooding the rural passenger transport market. Lack of effective supervision of the rural passenger transport market, the market order is chaotic.

(5) Production and operation is difficult. Rural passenger transport operating costs are high, the source of passengers scattered, unstable passenger flow, a considerable part of the rural passenger transport vehicles operating in difficulty.

(6) Single operation mode. Most rural passenger vehicles take the "fixed point, timing, fixed class, fixed line" class operation mode, a single mode of operation, cannot meet the needs of the rural masses in many aspects of travel. At the same time, the phenomenon of vehicles operating on a dependency is very serious, a small number of individual operations, the degree of organization of transport is not high.

(7) The vehicle equipment level is low. Most of them are ordinary buses, the proportion of middle and senior buses is small, and the technical level is low, the vehicle grade is poor, the vehicle is old and aging. Service facilities are not complete, there are greater safety risks, the quality of transport services is not high.

2.4　Rural passenger transport development policy guidance

1. Further improve ideological awareness

Rural passenger transport is the basic mode of transportation that the majority of farmers rely on for motorized travel, which is closely related to the production and life of farmers and social public welfare undertakings and livelihood projects, and it is the bridge and link between urban and rural areas. Accelerate the development of rural passenger transport, improve the access rate and service level, is to protect the basic needs of the masses to travel in a car, and promote the specific actions of the equalization of public services in urban and rural areas. It is important to serve the construction of a new socialist countryside, agricultural modernization and improve the income of farmers.

In recent years, China's rural transport infrastructure has improved significantly, the rural passenger transport access rate and service levels continue to improve, the problem of difficult travel for farmers has been basically solved. However, due to China's vast territory, uneven economic development, complex natural geographic conditions in rural areas, farmers living in scattered and other factors, the problem of difficult travel for farmers has not been fundamentally resolved. Some areas are still not open to buses due to inadequate infrastructure. Some areas are still not open to buses or have opened the rural passenger transport lines can not operate normally because of the scattered passenger flow and insufficient policy protection. Some areas of rural passenger transport lines safety hazards are prominent. Transportation departments at all levels should fully understand the significance of further accelerating the development of rural passenger transport, effectively enhance the sense of responsibility, urgency and sense of mission, actively joint relevant departments to accelerate the improvement of institutional mechanisms and policy measures for the development of rural passenger transport, and constantly improve the rate of access to rural passenger transport and service levels to better meet the travel needs of the peasants.

2. Further accelerate the construction of rural passenger transport infrastructure

Local transportation authorities should conduct in-depth research on the travel needs and travel characteristics of the local farmers, integrated planning and accelerate the construction of rural highway and rural passenger transport stations and other infrastructure, the construction of infrastructure to be included in the transport key project plan. First, accelerate the construction and upgrading of rural highway. Vigorously promote the renovation and extension of rural highway, networking projects and the construction of slips and bridges, increase the transformation of dangerous bridges in rural areas, accelerate the completion of the task of hardening highway in the western region and concentrated special hardship areas, accelerate the upgrading of existing rural highway, strengthen the daily maintenance management, accelerate the formation of county highway as the backbone, rural highway as the basis of dry and branch connected, reasonable layout, safe and convenient rural highway network. Second, promote the "highway, station, transport" coordinated development. Coordinated planning and construction of rural highway and rural passenger transport station facilities, scientific planning and layout of rural passenger transport line network, promote rural passenger transport station and rural highway synchronous planning, synchronous design, synchronous construction, synchronous delivery, to ensure that "the highway is completed and smoothly open to traffic". Third, accelerate the construction of rural passenger transport stations. Increase investment in the construction of stations, according to the characteristics of local residents' travel demands, accelerate the construction of suitable standards, safe and practical township passenger transport stations, request stop, Harbor-shaped bus stop, etc., according to local conditions to determine the scale of construction of rural passenger transport stations. Fourth, promote the "passenger and cargo, transport and mail combination. Strengthen the cooperation with the supply and marketing sector and the postal sector, increase the logistics and postal service functions of rural passenger transport stations, give full play to the combination effect of rural passenger transport stations, vehicles in the service of rural logistics and rural postal, etc., and promote the integration and integrated development of rural passenger transport and rural logistics, rural postal.

3. Further increase support for the development of rural passenger transport

Local transportation authorities should actively coordinate with relevant departments, adhere to the positioning of basic public services of rural passenger transport, and constantly increase policy support to ensure that rural passenger transport to open, stay and benefit. First, to promote the establishment of public financial security system for rural passenger transport. Local transport authorities should actively report to the local people's government, and actively cooperate with relevant departments to promote the establishment of public financial security system for rural passenger transport. Increase public financial support, establish a stable funding channel. Local transport authorities can take the form of "subsidies in lieu of prizes", and support for the construction of rural passenger transport stations, vehicle updates, safety and security. Second, improve tax and fee support policies. Local transportation authorities should actively coordinate with relevant departments to promote the implementation of national policies on supporting rural passenger transport operators, rural passenger transport infrastructure construction of various subsidies and tax incentives, and improve the long-term subsidy mechanism. Local transportation authorities should do a good job of urban and rural highway passenger transport subsidies for refined oil price policy implementation and data statistics, funds issued and other work. Research and develop the county bus vehicles enjoy the same treatment and preferential policies with urban bus vehicles. Joint relevant departments to rural passenger transport of all kinds of charges for a comprehensive cleanup, and effectively reduce the burden on operators.

4. Further enhance the safety and security capacity of rural passenger transport

Local transportation authorities should attach great importance to the safety and security of rural passenger transport work, to take comprehensive measures to increase safety prevention and control efforts to effectively improve the level of safety of rural passenger transport operations. First, the implementation of the main responsibility for enterprise safety production. Adhere to the enterprise as the main responsibility for the safe operation, requiring rural passenger transport business enterprises regardless of the mode of operation, must assume first responsibility for the safe operation of its vehicles and drivers. Urged enterprises to strictly implement job responsibilities and safety system, the vehicles for the unified organization of scheduling. Promote driver quality education project, strengthen the driver qualification assessment and training. Second, improve the safety level of rural highway. Local transportation authorities continue to implement in-depth rural highway security projects, improve the technical standards of rural highway safety, increase the construction of rural highway security facilities and renovation efforts to improve the technical level of rural highway. Third, strengthen the audit of the conditions of passage. Fourth, strengthen the technical management of vehicles. Local transportation authorities to promote the standardization of rural passenger vehicles, and actively promote suitable for rural traffic conditions of affordable and environmentally friendly models to ensure that the vehicle safety and technical condition up to standard. Actively promote the application of rural passenger transport vehicle video surveillance and satellite positioning devices and other facilities and equipment, and urge enterprises to strengthen the dynamic monitoring of vehicle operations, improve vehicle safety and technical level.

5. Establish a dynamic monitoring mechanism for rural passenger transport access

Local transportation authorities should actively coordinate with relevant departments to establish a dynamic monitoring mechanism for rural passenger transport access, and constantly increase the supervision and inspection of the development of rural passenger transport. First, establish a monthly reporting system for rural passenger transport access. The provincial transportation authorities to speed up the establishment of the monthly reporting system of rural passenger transport access, clear responsible departments, designated special personnel, and seriously do a good job of rural passenger transport access rate statistics, surveys, verification and other work. Second, strengthen the supervision and evaluation of rural passenger transport access. Transportation authorities at all levels to strengthen the supervision and inspection of rural passenger transport access, take field verification, focus on random checks and other forms of rural passenger transport access to their regions for supervision and guidance. Establish a smooth complaint channel to accept the supervision of the masses. Actively strive to include the rural passenger transport access situation into the local well-off society construction goals, give recognition and funding to areas and units with outstanding achievements in rural passenger transport development, form an incentive and restraint mechanism to fully mobilize governments at all levels and relevant units to develop the enthusiasm and initiative of rural passenger transport.

2.5 Development trend of rural passenger transport in the new period

The development of low-carbon transportation in developed countries is mainly devoted to the innovation of transportation means and fuels to reduce carbon emissions, while in the process of development, we should pay more attention to the realization of single transportation mode efficiency improvement, transportation structure optimization, effective regulation of traffic demand, transportation organization and management innovation measures. Through the rational arrangement of transportation modes and layout, people will choose more public transportation and personal transportation such as walking and bicycling to achieve the reconstruction of the priority of urban and rural residents' travel modes, so as to curb the rapid growth of energy consumption and carbon emissions caused by the rapid growth of motorization.

For the vast rural areas in China, rural highway passenger transport is the most important way for rural residents to travel. In the case of limited funds, as far as possible to choose safe, reliable, economical and applicable rural passenger transport vehicles. How to form an intensive rural passenger transportation layout system with reasonable layout, close connection, convenience and orderly flow is the key to the green and low-carbon and sustainable development of rural passenger transportation in China. Focus on the following four aspects to explore the construction of rural passenger transport development system.

1. Traffic demand adjustment

Traffic demand management is a concept and idea of traffic management that actively controls the occurrence of traffic demand, actively guides the spatial and temporal distribution state of demand, and actively finds the balance point of traffic supply and demand relationship [10]. The idea of demand management is used to build and develop the rural passenger transport system, and through the effective guidance and regulation of rural residents' traffic behavior patterns and consumption concepts, the inefficient and unreasonable traffic demand is reduced and the sustainable development of transportation is realized. An efficient rural passenger transport system should play a central role in the daily travel of rural residents, gradually attracting passenger flow through perfect infrastructure conditions, efficient transport efficiency and good service level, guiding rural residents to travel in public and reducing travel by high energy-consuming transport modes.

2. Optimization of transportation structure

The optimization of transportation structure is to realize the service of rural passenger transport network, including the optimization of both transport network and transport mode. Transport network needs to strengthen the network construction of rural transport infrastructure, and build a perfect layout system of rural passenger transport network. While improving the coverage and access depth of the passenger transport network, we optimize the configuration of passenger transport lines, realize the reasonable organization of the network space, and effectively connect trunk lines with branch lines. Adopt reasonable operation organization mode to realize the high efficiency of passenger line operation. The optimization of transportation mode is for different distances, different levels of transport services for passenger demand. The passenger transport network is set up in different categories and levels, and multiple modes are combined to achieve complementary advantages and enhance transport efficiency.

Construct integrated passenger transport field station system, the rural passenger transport comprehensive field station for classification, grade, the passenger transport line along the stop site arrangement and optimization, promote the comprehensive use of land and functional development based on the site facilities, improve site coverage of the population rate. Key townships and passenger distribution centers should be built with a certain scale and level of passenger transportation field facilities, the rest of the towns, villages and factories, markets and other distribution points along the way need to set up waiting facilities or Harbor-shaped bus stop. Passenger lines set the first and last station, the formation of intensive, efficient rural passenger transport hub connection system, to promote rural passenger transport.

3. Transportation mode efficiency improvement

The energy consumption, emissions and transport capacity of various modes of transport vary. Even within the same mode of transportation, the energy consumption and emissions per unit of transportation can vary greatly due to different means of transportation, different fuels, and different operators. To achieve the low-carbon goal of rural passenger transport, we can start with the improvement of passenger vehicle transport efficiency, eliminate old vehicles, vigorously develop safe, practical and economic buses suitable for rural passenger transport, and train bus drivers on energy-saving operation to achieve the improvement of passenger transport efficiency.

4. Innovation of organizational management system

The scientific and reasonable capacity allocation and passenger transportation organization system controls the overall development scale of passenger vehicles. According to the characteristics of rural residents to travel passenger flow to dynamically allocate capacity, to achieve regionalization of capacity allocation and improve the level of regional coordination of rural passenger vehicles and the effectiveness of travel organization. Strictly implement fuel consumption limit standards for operating vehicles, and promote the construction of energy-saving and emission reduction management systems for the passenger transport industry. Establish an industry low-carbon assessment and accounting system to monitor energy conservation and emission reduction in the passenger transport industry. Unify the main body of rural passenger transport management, play a guiding role in the passenger transport industry authorities, clarify management responsibilities and regulate the operation of rural passenger transport.

2.6   Conclusions of this chapter

This chapter first introduces transport-related concepts, including rural highway, rural passenger transport, rural passenger flow, demand-responsive rural public transport, rural residents' travel, and travel demand, and carefully and meticulously elaborates each concept. Immediately after, this chapter introduces the current situation of rural passenger transport development, including the accelerated process of rural passenger transport network, the gradual construction and improvement of passenger transport stations, the gradual optimization of vehicle structure, the improvement of passenger transport organization and management and the improvement of passenger transport market order. Secondly, this chapter elaborates the outstanding problems in the current development of rural passenger transport and further analyzes the key factors that restrict the development of rural passenger transport. Then, the policy orientation of rural passenger transport development is interpreted, and support is sought from policies to strengthen the confidence in developing rural passenger transport. Finally, the trends of rural passenger transportation development in the new era are explained in the context of national policies, mainly including the more mature regulation of traffic demand, the more optimized transportation structure, the significant improvement in the efficiency of transportation modes, and the realization of new innovations in the organizational management system.

2.7 References

[1]   Bo Li. Research on western mountainous rural passenger capacity configuration[D]. Chongqing: Chongqing Jiaotong University, 2013.

[2]   Peishan Jiang. Study on rural passenger transport development planning[D]. Chengdu: Southwest Jiaotong University, 2009.

[3]   Ministry of Transport of the People's Republic of China. Road passenger transport and passenger station management regulations[S]. Beijin: Ministry of Transport of the People's Republic of China, 2015, 10.

[4]   Ruimin Shan. Policy Research For Rural Highway Passenger Transport in China [D]. Jilin University, 2007.

[5]   Wei Wang, Xiucheng Guo. Traffic Engineering [M]. Nanjin: Southeast University Press, 2003.

[6]   Yulong Pei, Hongping Li. Urban traffic planning [M]. Beijin: Chinese Railroad Publishing house, 2007.

[7]   Prbahat Shrivastava, S. L. Dhingra, P.J. Gundaliya. Application of Genetic Algorithm For Seheduling And Seheudle Coordination Problems[J]. Journal of Advanced Transportation.

[8] Xuefang Jiang. Behavior-based traffic trip prediction [D]. Xi'an: Xi'an University of Architecture and Technology, 2006.

[9] Wei Luo. Research on Prediction of Rural Passenger of Chongqing[D]. Chongqing: Chongqing Jiaotong University, 2011.

[10] Jianmin Xu. Traffic management and control[M]. Beijin: China Communications Press, 2007.

Chapter 3

Rural passenger flow analysis

3.1 Source of passenger flow

With the rapid development of the rural economy and the enhancement of urban radiation, the economic, material, and cultural exchanges between urban and rural areas have also been further expanded, and the role of rural passenger transport has also been further strengthened. Different from the urban passenger flow, the rural passenger flow mainly has the following characteristics:

(1) The urban industrial economy is developed, especially the increase in urban construction in recent years has provided a large number of jobs for the rural surplus labor, which constitutes the main source of rural passenger transport.

(2) Rural industries are strongly supported by the state, and

peasant go to cities to sell food, vegetables and other commodities, which is another important source of urban and rural passenger flow.

(3) After the improvement of peasant's economic and living standards, the frequency of going to the city for leisure shopping, visiting relatives, and seeking medical treatment has been increasing.

(4) The rapid development of township enterprises has brought frequent exchanges between urban and rural areas.

(5) Leisure activities such as "farmhouse" have become a way for urban residents to relax and travel, and this has also become an integral part of the rural passenger flow.

3.2 Characteristics of rural passenger transport

1. Public welfare of rural passenger transport

Similar to urban public transportation passenger transport, rural passenger transport is a short-distance passenger transport that provides services for the travel of the broad masses of peasant. Therefore, it also enjoys government policy support and fuel fee subsidies, and which has a certain public welfare nature. The nature of public welfare determines that rural passenger transport must be mainly invested by the government, and the funds for the development of rural passenger transport that benefit the broad masses of peasant should be included in the national and local government budgets. Institutionalize subsidies and compensation, and truly implement various financial subsidies, so that the broad masses of peasant can enjoy equalized services of a public welfare nature.

2. The dispersion of rural tourists

Dispersion refers to the inconcentration of the place of travel due to the inconcentration of the residential areas of the rural people. There are two main reasons for this dispersion: First, the rural areas are vast and the population living distribution is relatively scattered, so the rural masses travel more scattered and not concentrated. Secondly, the mountainous villages in the northwest are located in the deep hills or mountains, and the travel conditions are limited (far from the bus stop, the road access conditions are not good enough), so peasant masses travel less frequently, flow less, and source of tourists is less and unstable. In addition, because the mountainous area of northwest China is wide and sparsely populated, the villages are scattered and the roads in rural mountainous areas are poor, and the accessibility rate of rural roads cannot guarantee the convenience of transportation for all peasant. Therefore, after the opening of the rural passenger transport line, it appears that the towns and villages that some routes pass through have a large population of people, and the passenger transport volume is large, and overloading occurs during peak periods, which is a "hotline". On the contrary, the remote towns and villages through which some lines pass have relatively scattered population and small passenger volume, which leads to the vacant state of passenger transport vehicles in most of the time and a high vacancy rate, resulting in the waste of most transport resources.

3. The concomitant nature of regardless of passengers and goods

Concomitance refers to the characteristics of the simultaneous appearance, existence and disappearance of people and goods when rural residents travel. Because the main purpose of the rural population to travel in the mountainous areas of the northwest is to go to the market to buy means of production or living or trade agricultural products, they always travel with some commodities, which requires the rural passenger vehicles to carry passengers and storage space to carry goods.

4. High energy consumption of passenger transport tools

High energy consumption refers to the high loss of rural passenger transport vehicles during operation. Due to the low level of roads in the mountainous areas in the northwest, and even some other roads, the road width is narrow, the curves are many and sharp, the driving speed is low, the parts are worn out, and the fuel consumption is high. Therefore, high energy consumption will cause the cost of rural passenger transport to be higher than other passenger transport costs.

5. Volatility of passenger flows

Time volatility refers to the fluctuation of rural passenger flow over time. The time volatility is mainly due to the following two reasons: First, the frequency of peasant's travel during the slack and busy periods is different, so there will be different passenger flows in different seasons or during the slack and busy periods. In addition, there will be a certain fluctuation in passenger flow alternately when going to fairs in rural areas every few days. Second, there are a large number of ethnic minorities living in the mountainous provinces of the northwest. Various folk festivals, fairs, weddings and other festivals will bring a large number of "traveling villages and streets", visiting relatives and friends, and forming a festive passenger flow.

6. Orderliness of passenger flows

The orderliness of the outflow of passengers means that the peasant masses travel regularly in time. Due to the fact that a lot of peasant enter the city to work during the slack time, there is a flow of passengers entering the city in the morning and a flow of passengers returning from the city in the evening, and the time is relatively fixed, which forms a relatively stable and orderly passenger flow.

7. High risk of passenger transport

The high risk of rural passenger transport refers to the high risk of rural passenger transport during passenger transportation. Limited by the complex terrain and topography, the rural roads in the northwest mountainous areas generally have poor driving conditions, with low road grades, low pavement technical grades and many bends. Therefore, it will bring great safety hazards to traffic, i.e., rural passenger transport has a higher risk.

8. The network nature of passenger transport lines

Because the rural passenger line is laid along the low-grade roads in the countryside. The rural road network is crisscrossed, connecting the townships, towns, and villages scattered in different areas of the countryside. Therefore, the establishment of a rural highway network passenger transport line has the nature of a network.

3.3 Analysis on the influencing factors of rural passenger transport

In the development of rural passenger transport, the economic level reflects the ability of rural residents to pay and is a key factor in determining the passenger transport volume. The indicator can be expressed by GDP. The increase or decrease of the population will also directly affect the changes in passenger transport. At the same time, changes that affect rural passenger transport also include industrial structure, policy factors, etc. [1-2].

3.3.1 Demographic factors

The growth of rural population and changes in population structure are direct factors that affect rural passenger transport demand. Historical data shows that under a certain level of economic development, population growth, especially rural population growth, these will inevitably lead to an increase in demand for road passenger transport. At the same time, the adjustment and change of the population structure will inevitably lead to an increase in the demand for road passenger transport. In terms of the age and structure of rural population, the majority of rural road transport demand is the working-age population and the economically productive population aged 15-64. Among them, young people are the most active part of the population because they are energetic and active and they have a greater demand for road transportation. With the development of rural productivity and the transfer of rural surplus labor to cities and towns, the number of rural population has a greater impact on rural road passenger transport. At present, the elderly and children account for a relatively large proportion of the rural areas. Most young and middle-aged people go to school or work. Children can be divided into students and children under school age. Students include elementary school students, junior high school students, and high school students. Among them, because the school is close to home, elementary school students generally do not go to school by car, but they are escorted to school by their parents by bicycle or walking. Junior high school students and high school students are far away from school, so they usually go to school by car, and a small number of them are escorted to school by their parents driving or biking. This part of the students' travel has obvious regularity and periodicity. The elderly generally seldom travel, the scope of activities is generally the village where they are located, and their travels are generally on market days. Therefore, the impact of rural population on rural passenger transport cannot be ignored, and rural population can be used as the main factor influencing rural passenger transport.

3.3.2 Economic level

Transport and economic development are inseparable. Economic development brings greater demand for transport and promotes the further development of transport. In economics, GDP is often used to measure the comprehensive level of economic development of the country or region. This is the most concerned statistics in the macro economy, so it is considered to be the most important indicator to measure the development of the national economy. The level of rural economic development and the living standards of peasant are one of the important factors affecting the demand for rural passenger transport. Agriculture accounts for a large part of China's economic structure. Especially in recent years, with the development of the rural economy, particularly the rapid development of township and village enterprises, there have been frequent exchanges of personnel and materials between towns and towns, and between towns and cities. Especially with the specialization, commercialization, modernization of the rural economy, and the development of rural urbanization, a large number of rural surplus labors have been liberated and their transfer to cities and towns has increased, which puts forward a higher demand for road transportation. The continuous improvement of peasant's material and cultural living standards and the substantial increase in per capita income have greatly enhanced people's ability to pay for road transportation, which puts forward a higher demand for rural road transport.

At the same time, due to the continuous improvement of the economic level of rural residents, a small number of villagers already own their own cars, and travel problems can be solved by themselves. Most villagers also have their own electric cars or motorcycles, especially middle-aged people who stay in the countryside. Only a small number of people do not own travel tools such as cars or electric vehicles. Therefore, how to make the travel of these people easier and more comfortable is a major issue that this book will study.

3.3.3 Industrial structure factor

The adjustment of rural industrial structure and productivity layout is also an important factor affecting rural passenger transport demand. With the optimization of the rural industrial structure, the rapid development of high-efficiency agriculture, ecological agriculture, export agriculture, and high-quality agricultural products, as well as the acceleration of the development of large-scale rural industries, new and higher requirements will be put forward on the quality of transportation services. In recent years, the agricultural production conditions of my country have steadily improved, the adjustment of the agricultural economic structure has increased year by year, and the process of agricultural industrialization has accelerated. The main manifestations are as follows: First, the progress of agricultural product production is concentrated in advantageous areas; second, the quality of agricultural products is further improved. The optimization of the industrial structure has led to an improvement in the employment situation of rural labor transfers, and the number of rural labor transfers brought about by entering cities for work has increased significantly. The ever-increasing floating population has also become an important factor affecting the demand for rural passenger transport.

3.3.4 Urbanization construction factors

Urban construction also has a great impact on the demand for rural road passenger transport. In accordance with the requirements of urban-rural integration, formulate overall plans for the development of small towns in different regions, forming an urban-rural system structure of "central city-central town-general organic town-central village-grassroots village" in my country. With the acceleration of the pace of urban construction, the level of urbanization has further improved, and the rapid development of urban-rural integration. The further development and expansion of material and cultural exchanges and economic and technological cooperation between central towns and suburban counties, between counties and counties, and between counties and villages and towns. For the road transportation mode that connects these urban groups, the demand for passenger transport will surely maintain a certain growth rate.

3.3.5 Policy factors

National policies have the most direct impact on rural road transport demand. For example, the adjustment of road freight rates and the implementation of macro-policies for urban-rural integration construction have had a significant impact on rural road passenger transport. Mainly manifested in the following aspects:

(1) The impact of freight rates. There is a close relationship between the transportation demand of rural road passengers and the freight rate. Generally speaking, the provision of freight rate will reduce the travel demand; while the price drop will increase the travel demand.

(2) The impact of government investment. Under certain economic conditions, the amount of rural road transportation investment has a positive correlation with rural road transportation demand. Basically, rural road transportation investment increases, transportation capacity

increases, and transportation demand increases; otherwise, the opposite is true.

(3) The impact of policies. Local governments have introduced a series of preferential policies or policies to support the development of rural passenger transport in accordance with the actual conditions of the region. For example: Chongqing Municipality formulated and promulgated the "Chongqing Municipal-level Rural Passenger Transport Development Special Fund Management Measures." The establishment of the city's rural passenger transport development special fund subsidy method and use system will provide direct subsidy policies for rural passenger vehicles from towns to administrative villages and from administrative villages to administrative villages. This is conducive to reducing the cost of operators, and the preferential policies directly reflect the fares of rural passenger transport, which promotes the growth of rural passenger transport demand.

(4) The implementation of the macro policy of urban-rural integration construction, urban-rural integration construction has promoted the acceleration of rural urbanization, and the exchange of materials, personnel and technology has increased the demand for rural road passenger transport [3].

3.3.6 Factors of popularity of networking and acceptance by villagers

With the rapid development of today's society, networked informatization and digitalization have been heated up. Networking has indeed brought us many conveniences, such as online shopping, online trading, and online office. It can be said that networking has become a routine operation in cities and has become an indispensable part of the lives of urban residents. It has formed the phenomenon that things that can be solved by the network and which are not going out as much as possible. However, in rural areas where there are a large number of elderly and left-behind children, is networking equally popular? The answer may not be so ideal. Due to differences in ideological concepts and lifestyles, it may take longer for rural residents to have the same acceptance as urban residents. First of all, we must solve the ideological problem, how to convince rural residents that some things in life can be solved through networking, and let rural residents experience that the purpose of traveling through mobile phones can be achieved through tangible conveniences. Therefore, the popularity of networking and the acceptance of rural residents are the major factors that really restrict demand-responsive rural passenger transport services.

3.4 Travel characteristics of rural residents

The level of social and economic development largely determines the travel characteristics of residents in a region, and this is also applicable to the study of travel characteristics of rural residents in remote mountainous areas in northwest China. The social and economic development of the rural areas in the mountainous areas of the northwest lags far behind the eastern coastal and northern plains, so the rural residents in the northwest have their own characteristics. Among them, the factors that affect the travel characteristics of rural residents include local customs, living habits and income levels. The travel characteristics of rural residents mainly include the age composition and purpose of travel.

Unlike urban residents, rural residents in the northern plains, and coastal rural residents, the travel purpose of rural residents in the mountainous areas of the northwest is relatively single, and there is only one general travel purpose. Moreover, almost all travel modes are directly or indirectly related to agricultural production and life, and the main travel needs are still original. Mainly there are going to work, visiting relatives and friends on holidays, shopping on "market days" and selling agricultural products, going to the city to see a doctor, doing business, etc. The simple travel structure of rural residents shows that under normal circumstances, the vast majority of migrant workers are middle-aged and young men, while the travels to visit relatives and friends are mainly the elderly, women and children.

From the perspective of age composition, the daily travel in the northwestern mountainous rural areas is mainly elderly and children. Because in the economically backward rural areas, most of the young and middle-aged people choose to go out to work in order to earn money to support their families. Rural primary and middle school students commuting to and from school take up a relatively large proportion of their usual daily travel, while the smallest proportion of travel subjects are elderly people over 70 years old and children younger than 10 years old. During peak holiday periods, the travel share of each age group varies accordingly.

The purpose of travel refers to the purpose to be achieved during a travel. Analyze according to different travel time periods: During the peak period, the main travel objects are the elderly, middle-aged and young people, teenagers, students, and children. The purpose of travel is also relatively simple, mainly consisting of going to the city for work, going to the city to do business, going to the city to purchase production materials, seeing a doctor, shopping and leisure, and other travel purposes. In the peak hours of holidays, the main travel objects are the elderly, middle-aged and young people, teenagers, and children. The purpose of travel is relatively diversified, consisting of travel purposes such as going to work in the city, going to school, visiting relatives, seeing a doctor, shopping and leisure, doing business and other travel purposes.

3.5 Passenger flow distribution characteristics of rural passenger transport lines

1. Line distribution characteristics

The rural passenger transport is divided into three levels: main trunk line, sub-trunk line and branch line. The intensity of passenger flow travel of different levels is very different, which constitutes the distribution characteristics of rural passenger transport lines. Among them, the passenger flow density that undertakes passenger transport between the central county and important towns is high, and the scale of passenger flow is the largest. The passenger flow of passenger transport lines between central towns and general towns is relatively small, while the passenger flow of passenger transport lines connecting remote administrative villages and central towns is the smallest. There are many factors influencing the spatial distribution characteristics of routes, which are generally closely related to the degree and distribution of population concentration, economic relevance and spatial accessibility.

2. The imbalance of time and space

Towns and villages in rural areas are gradually established with the population gathering, which has a certain randomness and dispersity. Therefore, the population distribution is not balanced in space, which makes the passenger flow dispersed. The imbalance of passenger flow in time is mainly due to the uncertainty of rural residents' travel behavior. For example, the passenger flow of rural residents traveling during holidays and daily travel is not balanced (the peak passenger flow entering the city in the morning, and the peak passenger flow out of the city at night). The source of tourists at different times is unstable, and there is a large travel demand on fixed "market days" or major festivals such as temple fairs, and an explosive passenger flow has emerged. In addition, the rural passenger flow will also show certain regular fluctuations in seasonal time.

3. Directional distribution characteristics

The directional distribution characteristics of passenger lines are mainly two-way and one-way types. The two-way type means that within a unit time period (generally 1 h), the amount of passenger flow on a certain passenger line is basically the same. The one-way type means that within a unit time period (usually 1 h), there is a large difference in passenger flow between the upstream and downstream of a passenger line. During peak hours, most passenger lines show a two-way pattern, while during peak hours, most passenger lines show a one-way pattern. The unidirectional asymmetry is mainly due to the characteristics of rural residents "entering the city in the morning and leaving the city in the evening" and the regular intervals of rural residents "going to market and returning to their hometowns".

The directional distribution imbalance of passenger flow is generally expressed by the directional imbalance coefficient [3], and its calculation formula is shown in formula (3.1):

$$D_r = 2Q_r / (Q_r + Q_r')$$ (3.1)

In the formula, Q_r represents the maximum cross-sectional passenger flow during peak hours in one direction, and the unit is: person/hour. Q_r' represents the maximum section passenger flow corresponding to Q_r, in person/hour. Generally, the of two-way line is 1.1-1.2, and the one-way line is 1.4-1.5.

4. Time distribution characteristics

The time distribution characteristics [4] are mainly manifested as the tidal nature of the rural passenger flow. It mainly presents the daily distribution characteristics of the morning peak in the morning and the evening peak out of the city in the evening, as well as the weekly distribution characteristics with a cycle of the market interval. In addition, the seasonal farming season goes to the city to buy the means of production and goes home to farm, while the farm slack season goes to the city to work, do business, leisure and entertainment, visit relatives, etc., which will form a monthly distribution characteristic of rural passenger flow.

The daily unevenness of passenger flow is expressed by the daily unevenness coefficient A, and its calculation formula is shown in formula (3.2):

$$D_t = \frac{Q_{max}}{\sum Q_i / h} \tag{3.2}$$

In the formula, Q_{max} represents the total passenger flow of the entire line during peak hours, the unit is person/hour, Q_i represents the passenger flow of the i-th hour, the unit is person/hour, and h represents the number of business hours throughout the day.

The seasonal unevenness of passenger flow is expressed by the seasonal unevenness coefficient D_s, and its calculation formula is shown in formula (3.3):

$$D_s = \frac{365 Q_t}{Q_t} \tag{3.3}$$

In the formula, Q_t represents the passenger flow during peak passenger flow t days, and the unit is person. Q represents the total annual passenger traffic of the statistical route, the unit is person/year.

5. Collection and distribution characteristics

In the middle of the rural passenger line, there are often some naturally formed temporary stops with a fixed source of passengers. The natural formation of these stops is related to the concentration of residents around the stops, the production and lifestyle of rural residents. In this paper, the distribution intensity [5] is used to quantitatively describe the importance of various distribution points in their service range, and the calculation formula is shown in formula (3.4):

$$S_i = \frac{q_i}{\sum_{i=1}^{n} X_i} \tag{3.4}$$

In the formula, S_i represents the concentration and distribution strength of the i-th gathering and distributing point. q_i represents the average daily number of passengers on and off at the i-th distribution point, $i = 1, 2, 3, ..., n$. n represents the total number of vehicles that started or passed at that point. X_i represents the authorized number of passengers for the i-th vehicle passing through the collection and distribution point.

3.6 Importance of passenger flow collection and distribution points on rural passenger transport lines

3.6.1 Classification and characteristics of collection and distribution nodes

The distribution of rural residential villages is scattered and messy, especially in the remote mountainous areas of northwest China. Therefore, the passenger flow distribution points along the rural passenger transport lines in these areas are often more random. However, through investigation, it is found that there are some fixed temporary stops for passengers to get on and off the line, namely fixed passenger flow distribution nodes, which mainly include the following common types:

(1) County passenger transport station.

(2) Township passenger transport station.

(3) Location of primary and secondary schools.

(4) Villages with a high degree of population agglomeration.

(5) Important enterprises.

(6) Conventional place.

3.6.2 Factors affecting the importance of collection and distribution nodes

1. Node size

The size of the node has an important influence on the importance of the node. We often take the area of the influence area of the collection and distribution passenger flow node in the route as a quantitative indicator of the node scale. Because the passenger volume of the collection and distribution node is related to the number of rural residents around the node. When the average residents' average travel intensity (the number of trips per capita) is the same, a node with a larger population has a greater demand for passenger transport, and the node has a stronger role in the entire rural passenger transport network. Therefore, the population scale is used to measure the scale of the node.

2. Resident income level

In terms of the nature of travel, residents' travel needs include two types of demand: intrinsic and derived. Intrinsic travel demand is a rigid demand in rural areas and has nothing to do with income level, while derivative demand has greater flexibility and is closely related to the income level of local rural residents. Generally speaking, the higher income level in rural areas, the higher derivative demand, which leads to a larger total travel demand in the entire region. And vice versa. With the continuous improvement of the income level of rural peasant in our country, the quality of life has also improved, and the proportion of rural travel demand for derivative travel in the total travel is also rising.

3. Industrial layout and land use form

The industrial layout and land use form refer to the distribution of the industry in the areas within the radiation area of each collection and distribution node along the passenger line and the form of the application land. It reflects the intensity and frequency of population travel in the areas affected by the node and the degree of contact with the node and the outside world.

4. Traffic accessibility

The rural passenger transport is based on the rural road network, so the traffic conditions of all levels of roads along the line are the prerequisite and foundation for the development of passenger transport, and it has a very important influence on the importance of rural passenger transport distribution nodes. Under normal circumstances, we use the accessibility of the node to measure the traffic condition of the collection and distribution node, that is, the number of roads and the road level through the node in the rural road network can be used to quantify this index.

5. Geographical location

The geographic location of each collection and distribution node in the rural passenger transport line is also very important to the importance of the node in the entire line. The geographic location of the collection and distribution node refers to the location of the node in the entire area, which has a direct impact on the importance of the node. Under the same conditions, the importance of the nodes located in the center of the area is greater than the importance of the nodes in the edge areas. According to the rural passenger transport network system, the rural passenger transport nodes can be divided into three levels: the first level is the start and end nodes of the lines of the passenger stops in the county towns in the central areas. The second level is the important township nodes along the route. The third level is the fixed passenger collection and distribution nodes along the route (primary and secondary schools, high-population villages, important factories and mines, large-scale agricultural and animal husbandry bases, and markets).

3.6.3 Importance of collection and distribution nodes

According to the distribution node and its various influencing factors, an appropriate evaluation method is selected to evaluate its importance. According to the goal to be achieved by the evaluation system and the relationship between the index system and the target layer, the simplex matrix method is usually used to evaluate the importance of each collection and distribution node: the importance of each collection and distribution node on a rural passenger transport line is evaluated. Suppose there are n fixed nodes $P_1, P_2, ..., P_n$ on this route, and m individual evaluation indicators $a_1, a_2, ..., a_m$ are selected from the influencing factors to construct discriminant matrices D and C_k. Calculate the weight of each indicator and the importance of each node. Check the consistency of the discriminant matrix D and C_k. Calculate comprehensive indicators.

For node $p_i (i = 1, 2, ..., n)$, its comprehensive evaluation index V_j is:

$$V_j = \sum_{i=1}^{m} W_i * V_{ij} \tag{3.5}$$

In the formula, W_i represents the weight of the i-th index, and V_{ij} represents the value of the j-th index of the i-th node. The greater calculated value of the comprehensive index V_j, the greater importance of the node. V_j is divided into 2 to 3 levels as an index of node importance. The first level is the central node in the rural passenger transport network, that is, the most important point in the collection and distribution node.

3.6.4 Attraction range of important collection and distribution nodes

The roads that constitute the rural passenger transport network in the mountainous areas of northwestern China are mainly second and lower roads, and there are also many substandard ways. The fixed collection and distribution nodes on the rural passenger transport network are mainly distributed in important towns, schools, factories and mines along the two-level passenger transport routes of the rural main road and secondary roads where passenger flow is generated and dissipated. Generally, these common node platforms where passengers pick up and drop off are usually in the form of simple platforms or signboards. For important township nodes, the passenger flow is mainly connected to the administrative village through the passenger branch line. This kind of branch line has fewer departures, large passenger flow fluctuations, great randomness, and small transportation capacity. Small minibuses with 6-12 seats are generally put on branch lines. According to the distance of the node's radiation range and the means of transportation used to reach it, the range of important collection and distribution nodes can be divided into three levels: one, two and three.

1. First-level attraction range

Walking is the only means of transportation to reach the important collection and distribution nodes along the main and secondary trunk lines of each rural passenger transport, that is, such residents live within the acceptable walking distance from the important collection and distribution nodes, often using 1 km as the boundary. Therefore, all those within 1km from the collection and distribution node belong to the first-level attraction range.

2. Second-level attraction range

The range of distances from small vans, tricycles, motorcycles, mopeds, etc., to important collection and distribution nodes along the rural primary and secondary passenger transport trunk lines is called the second-level attraction range. The second-level attraction range is an area of 1-3 km.

3. Third-level attraction range

The third-level attraction range refers to the distance range of the residents of administrative villages in the branch line passenger transportation of the rural passenger transport network through the village road branch line small minibus to the nearest township passenger station. The attraction range includes the entire areas of the village that can be included in the village branch line. The third-level attraction range is generally above 3 km.

In addition, the determination of the attraction range of the collection and distribution node in rural areas should also appropriately consider the topography, road network structure, land use form, industrial structure, travel expenses, etc. of different areas. Therefore, determining the range of attraction is a very complicated task, and the main influencing factors must be grasped from a macro perspective in order to reduce the calculation error.

3.7 Summary

This chapter first analyzes several sources of rural passenger flow, and at the same time analyzes several major characteristics of rural passenger transport. It includes the public welfare of rural passenger transport, the dispersion of rural passenger sources, the randomness of passenger and cargo, the high energy consumption of passenger transport tools, the fluctuation of passenger flow, the orderliness of passenger flow, the high risk of passenger transport, the network of passenger lines and so on. Secondly, it analyzes the factors that affect rural passenger traffic, and then analyzes the characteristics of rural residents' travel and the distribution characteristics of rural passenger line passenger flow. The passenger flow distribution characteristics include line distribution characteristics, temporal and spatial distribution characteristics, and collection and distribution characteristics. Finally, the concepts and calculation methods related to the importance of passenger flow collection and distribution points on rural passenger lines are explained, and the attraction range of important collection and distribution points is defined.

3.8   References

[1]   Ding Qing. Analysis of rural passenger transport market and influencing factors[J]. Neijiang Science and Technology, 2007(11): 59.

[2]   Thiel F. I. Social effects of modem highway transportation[J], Public Roads, 1962, 32(1): 1-10.

[3]   Xiang Wei. Research on the planning method of public transit between town and country[D]. NanJing: Southeast University, 2006.

[4]   Li Bo. Research on western mountainous rural passenger capacity configuration [D]. Chongqing: Chongqing Jiaotong University, 2013.

[5]   Wang Wei, Yang Xinmiao, Chen Xuewu. Urban public transportation system planning method and management technology[M]. Beijing: Science Press, 2002.

Chapter 4

Research on the planning and layout methods of rural passenger station

The rural passenger station is the basic link of the rural passenger transport system. It is an important place for the arrival and departure of vehicles and the gathering and dispersing of passengers. The normal function of the rural passenger station is the guarantee for the normal operation of the entire rural passenger transport system. Rural passenger transport stations play the role of collecting and distributing passengers, parking vehicles, and operating scheduling in the passenger transport market. They can effectively combine the interests of passengers, transport operators and transport management departments, attract and radiate economic activities in surrounding areas, promote the healthy and orderly development of rural road transportation, as an important part of the comprehensive transportation system in rural areas, rural passenger transport stations are optimized for the layout of rural passenger transport stations, which is conducive to building a smooth, efficient and convenient road transport system, improving the efficiency and organization of the entire transport system, to achieve the purpose of low-carbon transportation.

However, the tradition of focusing on construction and neglecting planning has resulted in uncoordinated layout, unreasonable scale, insufficient capacity, and inconsistent construction standards for rural passenger transport stations, and the functions of rural passenger transport stations have not been fully utilized. Therefore, it is necessary to determine a reasonable site selection and construction scale based on the scientific planning and layout of the rural township system. This chapter introduces the classification and layout methods of rural passenger transport stations in detail, analyzes the functions of various stations, and proposes the construction standards of the stations.

4.1 Planning and layout principles of rural passenger transport stations

Planning and layout principles of rural passenger transport stations are as follows[1]. It must be combined with the actual situation of rural land, comply with the requirements of the Ministry of Transport on the layout planning of rural passenger transport stations, implement the principle of simultaneous function, reasonable division of labor, coordinated development, and non-interference.

1. Adaptability principle

The development of the rural economy will directly affect the travel needs of rural residents, the travel needs of rural residents is the most important factor in the planning of rural passenger transport stations, in addition, demand-responsive rural buses are completely oriented towards passenger travel demand, therefore, the planning of rural passenger transport stations needs to consider the peculiarities of demand-responsive rural public transport services and the uncertainty of rural residents' travel, making rural station planning need to be extremely adaptable, on the one hand, the planning of rural passenger transport stations should fully consider the economic development trends of various districts, counties, towns, and administrative villages, and the planned layout of stations should be compatible with the layout of township settlements, on the other hand, it is necessary to combine the characteristics of rural residents' random trips, and reasonably select the location of passenger transport stations to meet the current and future needs of rural residents.

2. Coordination principle

With the acceleration of urbanization and the further expansion of urban space, the planning of rural passenger transport stations must be coordinated with the planning of towns, towns and villages, and meet the requirements of local development planning. Not only the planning of passenger transport stations must be consistent with urban development, but also the agglomeration effect of the construction of rural passenger transport stations on urban development.

3. The principle of proper advancement

Due to the particularity of demand-responsive rural public transport services, rural residents will travel more comfortably and more conveniently in the future, which can stimulate rural residents to increase travel to a certain extent, therefore, the layout planning of rural passenger transport stations must not only meet the needs of current social and economic development, but also have appropriate advancement, so that the planning can meet the needs of future passenger transport, and can be coordinated with the future regional economic development, but not too far ahead, causing a waste of resources.

4. Economic principle

In the site layout and site selection, full consideration should be given to the use of existing sites, saving construction funds by transforming and improving the original site land, facilities, and operating mechanism, which should ensure the passenger transportation capacity during the transition period, meet the requirements of combining the new with the old and gradually transition, and give full play to the operational capabilities of the existing stations.

5. Principles of environmental protection

Correctly handle the relationship between site construction and environmental protection. The site planning should meet the minimum damage to the ecological environment, maximize the service functions of the sites at all levels, realize the harmony between the development of transportation and nature, and promote the coordinated development of regional economy, society and the environment.

6. The principle of convenience for residents to travel

Due to the travel habit of rural residents, there will be some conventional waiting stations, for example, near the rural small shop, near the villager activity room, etc. These specific places are often places with a high concentration of villagers. Therefore, these places need to be fully considered in the site layout, and simple sites are arranged in these places, and the acceptance of villagers is often much higher.

4.2 Hierarchy and classification of rural passenger transport stations

4.2.1 Hierarchical system

The hierarchical system of rural passenger transport stations is mainly reflected in two aspects: functional level and technical level [2]. From the functional level, it is mainly divided into central town passenger station, general town passenger station, township and rural junction station, and village station, include villages and towns with conditions and relatively urgent demand for rural passenger transport stations into the central town passenger transport station, in terms of construction timing and construction standards, priority may be given to the need for further improvement of the economic development and traffic conditions of the central towns. In terms of technical level, the sites in each functional level are combined with the needs of each township to set up corresponding levels of sites, among them, the passenger stations in the central town are mainly level three and four, and the general passenger stations are mainly level four, five and simple stations. Rural sites are mainly simple ones, and each site needs to set up stop signs, which indicate the appointment telephone number, appointment software APP, appointment time and other related information.

According to investigations, some of the completed township passenger stations are in good operating conditions, while others are difficult to function, the latter is mainly due to the improper location of the passenger stations. Rural township passenger transport stations must be constructed according to their own actual conditions and in accordance with local conditions. In the central towns and villages in areas with strong social and economic strength, and some towns and villages are located in transportation hubs and tourist nodes, large-scale and high-level passenger stations should be built, some small towns without distribution functions, or towns that are not at traffic nodes, and some towns that are very close to each other and co-located on the same rapid transit line, can set up waiting sheds in the short term, and in the long term through combining demand changes gradually upgrade the level, and other areas can meet the station conditions for all township residents to travel by means of simple stations.

4.2.2 Site classification

The rural passenger transport station is an important part of the rural passenger transport system. It is an infrastructure that provides parking, ticket purchase, bus waiting, information services and other functions for rural passenger transport. In order to better reflect the differences in the functions of rural passenger transport stations, and to provide a basis for determining the functions, construction standards, and support policies of various stations, rural passenger stations can be divided into four categories.

1. Hub station

A hub station refers to a station where the trunk line and the trunk line, and the trunk line and other modes of transportation (urban buses, long-distance passenger shuttle buses, taxis, and rail transit, etc.) connect. Generally located in the central areas of the county or central town, it is the junction and transfer point of long and short distances, and the connection point with other modes of transportation. It has the characteristics of many lines and large passenger flow, there are functions such as ticket sales, waiting, parking, and vehicle inspection, such hub stations should be constructed in accordance with the standards of passenger stations above Class 4 [3].

2. Ordinary stations

Ordinary stations are generally located in ordinary towns and towns, and are usually the junctions of main lines and branch lines. Ordinary stations have more departure lines and a larger passenger flow, and have functions such as ticket sales, waiting, and departure. Constructed according to the standard of a five-level passenger station or a simple station.

3. Greeting station

It is located in an administrative village with a large population (such as the seat of the township government before the combined town) or a central administrative village, and has the functions of waiting and departing.

4. Shelter

Located in ordinary administrative villages, natural villages, rural arterial roads or rural roads along the customary pick-up and drop-off point of passengers, it has obvious station signs, can be set up with sun-shading and sheltering facilities, and can be built on roadside shops or public places. Bus shelters are divided into two categories: A and B according to their scale and function. Class A shelters refer to large-scale waiting trains with functions such as sheltering from the wind, rain and sun, resting and waiting, and line identification information (including the name of the rural passenger transport line that runs, the operating time, the name of the main village and town, the name of the station in the village, and the service supervision telephone, etc.) pavilion; Class B shelters are small shelters with only route identification information [3].

4.3 Site layout method

4.3.1 Layout method of hub station and ordinary station

The importance of the node has a strong correlation with the construction importance and scale of the rural passenger station in the area, the greater the importance of the node, the greater the importance of the construction of the rural passenger transport station, and the larger the scale of construction. The layout of the township hub station is based on the importance of the node, using quantitative and qualitative analysis methods. The layout of the hub station mainly solves two problems: one is the determination of the functional level of the passenger station, and another is the location of the passenger station [4].

1. Determining the scale and level of passenger transport stations

The layout planning of rural passenger transport stations is a complex systematic project, affected by various factors such as transportation, economy, population, and related development policies. The layout is usually carried out by a combination of quantitative calculation and qualitative analysis. Based on the important calculation of nodes, sort the nodes in order from high to low, and this study qualitatively analyze their transportation location, development policies and other factors. The greater the importance of the node, the more obvious the advantage of the transportation location, and the stronger the development policy, the higher the construction level of the node. Refer to the following standards for the construction grade scale of the hub station:

Traffic location theory [5] think: the traffic volume generated by the few (1/3) node cities in the area accounts for the majority (2/3) of the total traffic volume generated in the corresponding areas. Therefore, in the calculation of the scale of rural passenger transport stations, all the towns in the county area are used as transportation nodes, and the importance of each node is analyzed as a quantitative indicator of the passenger transport capacity of each township, so as to calculate the construction scale of each township passenger transport station [6].

The calculation method of the importance of each township node is to select the social economy and traffic evaluation indicators such as population, national income, tertiary industry value, and highway access rate, and use the analytic hierarchy process to determine the weight value of each indicator. In actual application, because the socio-economic statistics of each township is difficult to obtain, it is necessary to filter the indicators. According to the actual situation of social economy, urban development, population distribution, etc., three indicators of total population of each township, rural economic income, and average income of farmers can be selected as indicators for quantitative analysis of the importance of each node. The calculation formula of node importance is shown in the formula in Chapter 3.

2. Site selection of passenger transport stations

The location of ordinary passenger stations in towns and villages is different from that of central hub stations, and qualitative analysis methods are generally used for address selection. First of all, in order to achieve the goal of low-carbon transportation, the location of the township passenger station should be selected in accordance with the direction of the rural passenger transport line, pay attention to the connection with rural passenger transport lines to facilitate the transfer and transfer of rural residents, and its effective attraction range is within the acceptable range of rural residents' walking or cycling trips.

Secondly, the site selection process of the passenger station should be combined with the overall plan of the local town, with reference to the opinions of the land department and the transportation department, try to choose public welfare land, avoid occupying the existing construction land and other land with excessive compensation, pay attention to the protection and sustainable development of the ecological environment. In addition, the location of the passenger station gives priority to the original township transfer center. In order to meet the travel habits of rural residents as much as possible, and to ensure the continuity of passenger travel, the original transfer center can be modified and expanded. The occurrence and attraction of passenger flow are realized through stations. The choice of station site is also a key link in passenger transport network planning. The site selection of township passenger transport stations needs to consider the following factors:

① Investigate the availability of existing stations based on the principle of resource conservation, and try to use or rebuild existing stations as much as possible to save construction costs;

② There are available land resources, in addition to meeting current needs, it is necessary to reserve room for development to facilitate future expansion to meet future development needs;

③ The site selection should be coordinated with environmental development, and try to avoid neighboring residential areas, schools, hospitals and other areas that require a quiet environment;

④ Possess the necessary geological and engineering conditions to facilitate contact with the urban public engineering network;

⑤ The passenger station should be connected with the main roads of towns and towns as far as possible to avoid interference with urban traffic.

4.3.2 Layout method of greeting station and parking booth

Calling stations and bus shelters are the indispensable part of the rural passenger station system. The location and number of call stations and bus shelters will affect the convenience of residents' travel. Calling stations are generally located in large-scale administrative villages or central administrative villages, and bus shelters are generally located in general administrative villages or natural villages with rural passenger transport lines passing by. The setting of shelters and greeting stations should be based on actual conditions, consult local residents, and set up on the basis of an in-depth investigation of local residents' travel habits. The setting of greeting stations and bus shelters can follow the following principles:

(1) Administrative villages or natural villages with passenger lines passing through "Villages have stations or pavilions";

(2) Central administrative villages or administrative villages with large populations may consider setting up greeting stations, which have the function of departure. The types of greeting stations are determined according to actual conditions;

(3) For multiple natural villages densely distributed along the axis of the highway, call stations can be centralized, or multiple shelters can be set up according to residents' travel habits;

(4) For two or more natural villages that are distributed horizontally along the country road, and the passenger line cannot extend horizontally, Class A bus shelter can be set up near the road;

(5) If there are multiple village groups along the road, each village group shall set up a bus shelter. According to the actual situation of residents' travel habits, determine whether to set up Class A or Class B;

(6) The setting of shelters can be based on rural canteens or public places.

The facilities function and construction standards of rural passenger terminal stations are showed in Table 4.1.

Table 4.1　Facilities function and construction standards of rural passenger terminal

Site type	Function	Construction standards
Hub station	Usually located in the central area of the county or central town, it is the core of the rural passenger transport network, the junction of different levels of rural passenger transport networks, the transfer point of urban and rural passenger transport networks, the window from the countryside to the city, and the indispensable infrastructure of the rural passenger transport system. It has relatively complete station facilities and site facilities, with parking, waiting, transfer, ticket sales, maintenance, and repair functions	It is constructed in accordance with the standards of passenger transport stations above Level 4, and generally covers an area of no less than 2,000 square meters, and when conditions are restricted, no less than 1,500 square meters, with more than 2 parking spaces

Site type	Function	Construction standards
Ordinary station	Usually located in ordinary towns and towns, it is an effective supplement to passenger transport hubs, is the connection point between towns and between towns and villages, and is an important infrastructure for the rural passenger transport system. Have the necessary station facilities, with parking, waiting, transfer, ticket sales, maintenance and repair functions	Constructed in accordance with the standards of a five-level passenger station or a simple station, it should include necessary functional areas such as ticket halls, waiting rooms, toilets and management offices, with an area of not less than 60 square meters; the parking lot area is not less than 150 square meters, with more than 1 parking space; a security check area that can effectively park 1 medium-sized and above passenger car
Greeting station	Located in administrative villages with large populations or central administrative villages, it is an important passenger flow distribution point for the rural passenger transport network, an important support point for the passenger branch line, and the main infrastructure of the rural passenger transport system	Class A, the station building is not less than 30 square meters, should include waiting room, toilet and canteen, etc., with suitable parking and unloading positions and canopy; Class B shall include waiting signs beside the road and a port of at least 40 square meters composed of auxiliary roads, parking spaces and passenger pick-up and drop-off functions; Class C, with an appearance that meets the requirements, with suitable parking, pick-up and drop-off positions and canopies. The area and function settings refer to Class A
Shelter	It is located at the customary pick-up and drop-off point of passengers on rural arterial highways or along rural roads. It is the main support point for passenger flow of passenger transport lines and the main infrastructure of the rural passenger transport system	Class A shelter: 2.2 ~ 3 meters high, vertical projection area is no less than 12 square meters, and there is enough place for hanging line identification information; Class B shelters: 2.0-2.5 meters high, with a vertical projection area of not less than 0.3 square meters, and there is enough place for hanging line identification information

4.4 Summary

This chapter first introduces the principles of site layout planning, including adaptability, coordination, proper advancement, economy, environmental protection, and convenience for residents. Each principle plays a very important role in site layout planning. Only by integrating various principles and arranging the sites according to local conditions can maximize the benefits. Secondly, the level and classification of rural passenger transport stations are introduced, and the stations are divided into four categories: hub stations, ordinary stations, greeting stations, and bus shelters, and analysis of the setting of various stations. Finally, the layout method of the site is introduced. According to different site types, there are corresponding layout methods, which need to be laid out according to the functions of the site and the construction standards of the site.

4.5 References

[1] Cunye Lu. Research on development mode of rural passenger transport system under low-carbon economy[D]. Xi'an: Chang'an University, 2011.

[2] Hongguang Kang. Thoughts on the construction and management of rural passenger transport stations[J]. Highways & Transportation in Inner Mongolia, 2003(1): 44-45.

[3] Dayi Qu. AHP applied in priority order dicision highway network planning[J]. Journal of Highway and Transportation Research and Development, 2000(5): 102-106.

[4] Bo Zhang. A preliminary study on the public transport planning method of connecting villages. Hunan Communication Science and Technology[J], 2007(9): 184-187.

[5] Chudu Guan. Traffic location theory[M]. Beijing: China Communications Press, 2001.

[6] Wei Zhou. Optimizing items order of highway transport terminals based on analyzing importance of nodes[J]. Journal of Chang'an University (Natural Science Edition), 2006, 26(2): 69-72.

[7] Daoliang Liu. The status quo, management and development needs of rural passenger stations in my country[J]. Car and safety, 2013(8): 29-33.

Chapter 5

Research on the capacity allocation of rural passenger transport system

The rural passenger transport capacity discussed in this paper refers to the road line passenger transport capacity in the mountainous rural areas in the northwest. Specifically, the rural passenger transport capacity refers to the total passenger transport capacity provided by the passenger line vehicles specially serving rural residents in the rural road network. Generally speaking, the capacity allocation includes two parts: one is the capacity allocation of a single line, the other is the capacity allocation of a certain region or area. The rational allocation of rural passenger transport network is the requirement of the healthy and orderly development of rural passenger transport in the new era. Scientific and reasonable transport capacity allocation can not only bring convenience to residents, but also improve the efficiency of resources usage, passenger transport and economic benefits of enterprises.

5.1 Rural passenger transport operation mode

Operation mode of rural passenger transport [1]: Shuttle bus passenger transport has fixed lines, fixed stations, fixed shifts and fixed shift hours. Passengers can get on and off at the starting and ending points of the line and at each station along the way. There are two main types of passenger line operation: fixed shift operation and variable shift operation. Shift operation refers to the operation mode of strictly following the shift schedule on the specified line according to the shift time. There is no fixed schedule and fixed lines for the irregular shift operation. The operation of vehicles is arranged temporarily according to the actual passenger flow. The demand-responsive rural passenger transport in this study belongs to a special part of highway passenger transport. It is a mode of transport without fixed routes, fixed stations, fixed departure time, fixed models, fixed fares and fixed demands, and is a demand-oriented online reservation service mode.

5.2 Analysis of influencing factors of rural passenger transport capacity

There are two main types of factors affecting the allocation of rural passenger transport capacity, i.e., the total capacity influencing factors and the capacity structure influencing factors. Among them, total capacity influencing factors mainly include rural road passenger volume, transportation pricing, government policy guidance, etc., while the capacity structure influencing factors mainly involve government policy guidance, transportation distance, rural economic development and residents' income level and rural climate features, etc., and the structure diagram of the interrelationship between their various influencing factors are shown in Figure 5.1.

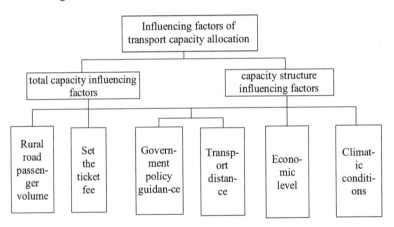

Fig. 5.1 Influencing factors of transport capacity allocation

1. Rural road passenger volume

Rural road passenger volume refers to the amount corresponding to passenger transport. Rural road passenger volume is directly related to the size of passenger transport capacity, which plays a decisive role. The rural passenger volume here refers to the future rural road passenger volume predicted according to the economic level, residents' travel frequency, land use and other factors. Whether it is urban bus passenger line or rural passenger line, the forecast result of passenger volume plays a decisive role in the capacity of the line. Conversely, in line operation, the rationality of planned transport capacity can be tested through the actual passenger volume in operation.

2. Government policy guidance

At present, the transportation industry in my country is still a monopoly industry dominated by the government transportation department. The development direction and trend of the transportation industry is also guided by the policies of the national government departments, that is, the rural passenger transport capacity is also inevitably affected by the government's macro policies. Government departments have a macro grasp of passenger transportation capacity allocation, organization and management, etc. Passenger transportation has a certain degree of public service, in order to guide the healthy, scientific and orderly development of the passenger transportation service industry.

3. Transportation distance

In the general agricultural slack season, the travel distance of rural residents is of the nature of short-to-medium distance. Because the lifestyle of rural residents is different from that of urban residents, travel time is often evenly distributed, and most of them are short-distance trips. When the travel distance is short, the waiting time that residents can tolerate is correspondingly shorter. Therefore, it is required that the capacity of short-distance passenger lines should be sufficient, passenger vehicles should have a high frequency of departure, and small and medium-sized vehicles should be the main ones with small passenger capacity. On the other hand, long-distance passenger lines can reduce the number of departments and improve the passenger carrying capacity of a single vehicle, and the transport capacity is mainly medium-sized vehicles. When transportation distances are long, residents can afford to wait longer. When transport distances are short, residents are reluctant to wait longer, so transport distances are an important factor to consider when allocating capacity. For short distance, the vehicle should be equipped with medium and small cars. For long distance, the frequency of departure can be adjusted appropriately, and the vehicle should be medium and large.

4. Fare setting

Different from the fixed fare of urban public transport, the main consumers of rural passenger transport are rural residents. The scattered source of rural passenger flow and the unstable passenger flow make rural passenger transport more expensive. Therefore, relative to the changes caused by the changes in freight rates, the sensitivity of transport capacity supply is greater than that of transport demand. The passenger ticket price is set too high, and the resulting effect is excess capacity, the decrease of the vehicle load rate, the high idle rate of passenger vehicles, the serious waste of transport resources, so that the operation cost is high, the profit is greatly reduced. On the contrary, it will stimulate the increase of travel demand, resulting in insufficient transport capacity, that is, it cannot well meet the travel demand of rural residents, and it will also damage the economic benefits of passenger transport enterprises. Therefore, too high or too low freight prices will lead to the waste of transportation resources, reduce the social and economic benefits of transportation. Therefore, maintaining a moderately elastic freight rate mechanism, through floating freight rate, can better alleviate the contradiction between supply and demand of freight capacity in a certain range, so as to achieve the purpose of rational allocation of freight resources.

5. Economic level

The level of regional economic development determines the ability of residents in the region to accept passenger transportation. Generally, in the northwestern region where the economy is relatively backward, when choosing a car model, it should be based on mid-to-upper-grade passenger cars. For the more developed coastal Yangtze River Delta or Pearl River Delta regions, higher-grade imported vehicles should be equipped with electronic display screens to provide various information services.

6. Climatic conditions

This factor has a slight impact on the structure of transport capacity. In northwest China, due to the large sand and relatively less vegetation, relatively appropriate vehicle color should be selected to ensure the comfort of service, and high strength window glass should be considered at the same time.

5.3 Vehicle model allocation

The level of rural road and the perfect degree of the infrastructure construction for the choice of model has a great influence, a reasonable model is conducive to make full use of rural road resources, improves transport efficiency, reduces the transportation cost, the choice of models to adapt to regional development stages and characteristics, different levels of economic development area models should not be the same, to avoid the pursuit of the city's image and increase the burden.

5.3.1 Principles of model selection

(1) According to the comprehensive line network level category and line service intensity, select reasonable models to meet the travel needs of passengers at all levels.

(2) According to the construction status of rural roads and the degree of perfection of transportation infrastructure, select reasonable models in order to give full play to the advantages of road resources and improve the efficiency of transportation.

(3) According to the needs of students commuting to and from school, residents commuting to and from get off work and traveling, corresponding car models can be specially equipped for the convenience of passengers.

(4) Due to the certain difference between urban and rural passenger transport and urban public transportation, the number of persons with rated load of the vehicle and various technical performances of the vehicle should be considered when selecting the vehicle type.

(5) According to the regional economic development level and local characteristics, develop models suitable for the city.

5.3.2 The general idea of model selection

The model selection is classified according to the level of the passenger transport network and the service nature of the trunk and branch lines, namely rural main passenger vehicles can be used in city bus technology standard models, and according to the rural traffic and frequency selection regional passenger car body structure form class line operation, models should choose accord with technical standards according to the traffic demand of small passenger cars, In addition, special vehicles can be configured to improve the pertinence and quality of services and meet special travel needs in order to meet the service requirements of specific routes such as tourist lines and night stay lines.

When selecting specific models, strictly implement fuel consumption limit standards for operating vehicles, accelerate the elimination of old passenger vehicles, encourage the selection of safe, practical and economic passenger buses suitable for rural passenger transport with low energy consumption and low emissions. Pay attention to the balance of vehicle prices and ticket prices, and pay attention to vehicle performance considering vehicle costs and the affordability of residents. On the premise of ensuring safety, improve ride comfort and adapt to the business mode of the enterprise, show the advantages of the model, establish the brand.

5.3.3 Specific criteria for model selection

Scientific and reasonable configuration of urban and rural passenger line network can not only make passengers travel more comfortable, safe and convenient, but also make each line operation benefit to achieve the best, which is of great significance to the development of passenger market. The selection of models should be based on the stage of development of regional passenger transport market, combined with local characteristics, and considering the characteristics of passenger flow of different levels of line network, select different passenger transport models, which can be mainly divided into passenger main line models, passenger sub-line models and branch models. Considering the function, nature, road conditions and people's travel characteristics of the operation line, the 8-meter level, medium and low floor is put on the urban and rural passenger trunk roads from the urban center to each township, and all kinds of auxiliary facilities including intelligent functions can be selected in the car. A bus with a single seat of about 15 and a passenger capacity of about 40. For the 19-seat medium-sized bus, which is put on the county general township line of passenger transport sub-line, the middle floor is equipped with sunshade, dismounting prompt system, electronic clock, and other auxiliary facilities such as computer stop announcers and coin-operated machine. For passenger transport sub-line important township an administrative village line, put in the body length between 3.5 meters to 4.8 meters, 10 seats below the small bus. Small passenger cars with body length between 3.5 meters and 4.8 meters and less than 10 seats are put on passenger feeder lines.

Because this book studies the demand response type rural passenger transport system, vehicle configuration needs to conform to the demand response to the needs of the rural passenger transportation way, due to different time period passenger demand is different, we can not accurately meet the needs and adapt to all of the models, and combined with local economic level and rural road conditions, the proposed large, medium and small three basic models. When the passenger demand in different time periods is closer to which type of vehicle, which type of vehicle will be selected for the passenger service in that period. In order to meet the needs of passengers on the premise of saving vehicle resources as much as possible. The specific vehicle configuration is shown in Table 5.1.

Tab. 5.1　Model configuration

Vehicle Model	Configuration
Large	The number of seats is about 20, and all kinds of functional auxiliary Settings can be selected in the car
Middle	The number of seats is about 15, and all kinds of functional auxiliary Settings can be selected in the car
Small	The number of seats is about 7, and all kinds of functional auxiliary Settings can be selected in the car

At the same time, in order to increase the recognition of car models, different colors can be set for different models of large, medium and small, so that the villagers can better distinguish them.

5.4　General Principles for Allocation of Rural Passenger Transport Capacity

In terms of capacity allocation, the principles of reasonable planning, quota control, strict qualification examination, pre-examination of car purchase, batch release, and intensive management should be followed [2]. In the process of capacity allocation, in order to avoid the phenomenon of hotline competition and abandonment of cold lines, the total capacity must be strictly controlled. The capacity allocation of a certain route for rural passenger transport should follow the following principles[3]:

1. The principle of meeting demand and being moderately ahead

In rural passenger transportation, there is a gradual gradual change in passenger transportation supply and frequent rapid fluctuations in demand, and it is difficult to maintain a relative balance between the two. In order to make the supply and demand of passenger transportation maintain a dynamic balance in the capacity configuration, the principle that the supply of passenger transportation capacity is moderately ahead of demand is adopted.

2. The principle of competitive competition and limited time use

For enterprises or individuals engaged in the operation of passenger transport lines, fair and equal quality bidding shall be conducted, and priority shall be given to good service quality. The operating lines are used for a limited period of time [4]. According to the assessment of the credibility of the operator, it is determined whether to continue to give a certain operation right.

3. The principle of reasonable and paid use of public resources

In order to reflect the utility of such resources as rural passenger transport lines, line operators must pay various fees (traffic fees, management fees, taxes, etc.) in accordance with regulations.

4. The principle of booking must be made for the ride

Since this book studies demand-responsive rural passenger transport services, all passengers who need to travel need to make reservations via telephone or online APP 24 hours in advance. By making an appointment, clarify the time of travel, the number of passengers traveling, the start and end points of the trip, etc., so that the bus company determines the schedule based on the above information.

5.5 Basic steps of rural passenger transport capacity allocation

For the allocation of passenger capacity of a rural passenger transport line, firstly, it is necessary to investigate and understand basic data such as economic development within the area affected by the passenger transport line, residents' income, and the operation of other passenger transport modes in the transportation corridor, and preliminary determination based on the predicted value of highway passenger transport volume. Capacity allocation for each characteristic year in the future. During the operation process, the total capacity and structure should be appropriately adjusted according to the actual situation to adapt to the actual needs of passenger transportation, so as to ensure the smooth development of passenger transportation. The specific configuration flow chart is shown in Figure 5.2.

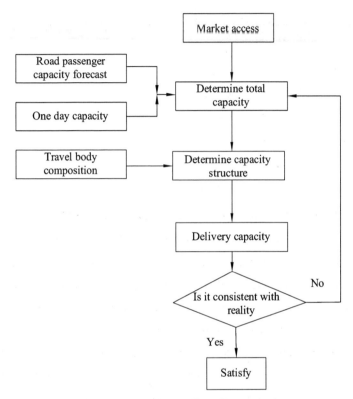

Fig. 5.2   Capacity configuration process

5.6   Research on the capacity allocation scale of rural passenger transport system

The capacity allocation of rural passenger transportation is mainly based on the demand of shuttle buses to determine the scale and size of the capacity. Its research mainly includes the study of the overall capacity scale configuration of the area and the study of the capacity configuration of a single line.

5.6.1 Calculation of the overall transport capacity of the area

Based on the imbalance of rural passenger transport capacity in northwest China, combined with the basic requirements of transport services and transport capacity allocation, the following calculation formula is proposed [5]:

$$Q_z = \frac{Q_d \cdot P \cdot L \cdot D_r \cdot D_s \cdot (1-\mu)}{m \cdot v \cdot k \cdot \alpha} \tag{5.1}$$

Where, Q_z represents the overall peak hour transport capacity of the region. Q_d represents the daily passenger volume (person-time/day) of rural passenger transport in the region. P represents the proportion of rush-hour passenger volume of rural passenger transport in the whole day passenger volume (%). L represents the average distance (km) of rural passenger transport in the region. D_r denotes the average direction non-uniformity coefficient of passenger flow in the area, generally 1.1-1.2. D_s denotes the seasonal non-uniformity coefficient of passenger flow in the area, generally not greater than 3. μ represents the allocation of transport capacity in an area, that is, the proportion of the number of vehicles saved in an area to the total number of vehicles allocated on a single line. m indicates the number of lines in peak hours. v represents the peak hour operation speed (km/h). k denotes the correction coefficient of operation speed in peak hours. In rural areas, the influence is relatively small and is generally 0.8-0.9. α represents the average coefficient of vehicle load at peak hours, which is generally recommended to be between 0.75 and 1.0.

5.6.2 Line capacity allocation calculation

The number of rural passenger vehicles is determined based on the peak hour passenger flow of a single passenger line, and its calculation formula is as follows [6]:

$$W = 2 \cdot \left(\frac{l}{v} + t_0 \right) \cdot n \qquad (5.2)$$

Where, W represents the maximum number of vehicles required by a single line in peak hours. l indicates the line length (km). v represents the vehicle operating speed (km/h). t_0 represents the one-way stop time (h). n represents the frequency of departures (per hour).

$$n = \frac{Q_h}{\varphi \cdot c} \qquad (5.3)$$

Where, Q_h represents the maximum passenger flow (person-time/hour) of the line in peak hours. φ represents the average vehicle load coefficient during peak hours. c represents the passenger capacity of the vehicle.

5.7 Research on the allocation of the demand-responsive rural passenger transport capacity

5.7.1 Capacity allocation ideas

Due to the particularity of the demand responsive rural bus service, its transport capacity configuration is different from that of the conventional bus or the conventional shuttle bus, so it is necessary to adjust and optimize the conventional bus or the conventional shuttle bus transport capacity configuration strategy on the basis of the development of the demand responsive rural bus transport capacity configuration strategy. The idea of rural public transport capacity allocation in demand response mode includes the following points: First, the passenger flow of each peak hour of the year should be obtained through prediction and combining with the actual situation; Secondly, select the maximum peak hour passenger flow in all days of the year, and use the calculation formula in Section 5.6 to solve the configuration number of standing demand response buses, which is the maximum number of demand response rural buses that need to be reserved in a certain period of time in this area. Finally, according to the passenger travel demand received every day, the genetic algorithm is used to solve the bus route optimization plan of every day, including the number of rural buses that need to be dispatched every day, the service station of each car and the number of service information.

5.7.2　Capacity allocation process

The entire process of demand-responsive rural public transport capacity allocation is very complicated and involves multiple technical points. This article aims to provide a way of thinking. In order to better show the steps of demand-responsive rural public transport capacity allocation, the form of flowchart is specially adopted, as shown in Figure 5.3.

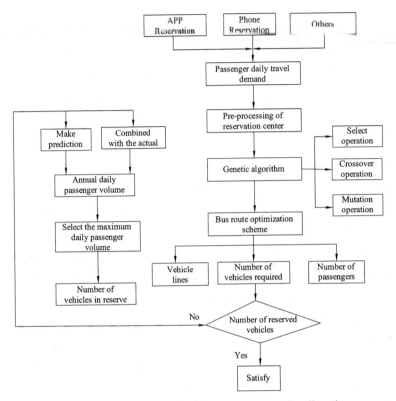

Fig. 5.3 Demand responsive rural public transport capacity allocation process

5.7.3 Route optimization model for capacity allocation

For rural residents, the purpose of travel is different. With the improvement of the economic level and the improvement of the level, the time concept of rural residents has become stronger and stronger. In the process of travel, it is not only to achieve the purpose of travel, but also to achieve the purpose of travel. The travel task is completed in the shortest time. Therefore, this paper pursues the optimization goal of the least total passenger travel time when constructing the demand-responsive rural bus route optimization model. From the perspective of the entire travel chain of passengers, the total travel time of passengers includes the time that the passengers are in the car and the time that the passengers are outside the car. Among them, the time that the passenger is in the car refers to the time when the passenger gets in the car to the time when the passenger gets off the car. The time up to 1 hour, the time a passenger is outside the car includes the time that it takes the passenger to arrive at the pick-up point from home, the time it takes to wait for the vehicle, and the time to get on and off the bus. There are three possible relationships between the time when passengers arrive at the station and the time when the vehicle arrives at the station. One is that the passenger arrives at the station before the vehicle, and there will be a waiting time. Second, the passenger and the vehicle arrive at the station at the same time, and the waiting time is not exist. Third, the vehicle arrives at the station before the passenger. At this time, since the passenger has not arrived yet, if the waiting time exceeds the limit, the vehicle will leave and the passenger cannot take this vehicle. Because it is difficult to use mathematical expressions to accurately describe the relationship between passengers and vehicles, in this article, the time when passengers are outside the vehicle only considers the time when passengers get on and off the vehicle.

The entire operation process of demand-responsive rural public transport includes four stages. In the first stage, the vehicle departs from the parking lot and arrives at the first boarding station; in the second stage, the vehicle serves all the boarding stations in turn according to the optimization strategy; In the third stage, the vehicle drove from the last boarding station to the first drop-off station; in the fourth stage, the vehicle served all the drop-off stations in turn; in the fifth stage, the vehicle drove back to the parking lot from the last drop-off station. Since there are no passengers in the first and fifth stages, they cannot be counted as the travel time of the passengers. The optimization model of the capacity allocation route is shown below.

$$\min Z = \frac{\sum_{k\in S}\sum_{i\in A}\sum_{j\in A} l_{ij}^k x_{ij}^k q_{ij}^k + \sum_{k\in S}\sum_{i\in A}\sum_{j\in B} l_{ij}^k x_{ij}^k q_{ij}^k + \sum_{k\in S}\sum_{i\in B}\sum_{j\in B} l_{ij}^k x_{ij}^k q_{ij}^k}{v} +$$

$$\sum_{k\in S}\sum_{i\in A\cup B} p_i ty_{ik}$$
(5.4)

$$x_{ij}^k = 1; \forall k \in S, \forall i \in A, \forall j \in B \tag{5.5}$$

$$\sum_{i\in A} p_i = \sum_{i\in B} p_i \leqslant k_{\max} Q \tag{5.6}$$

$$y_{ik} = 1; \forall i \in A \cup B, k \in S \tag{5.7}$$

$$p_i \leqslant Q; \forall i \in A \cup B \tag{5.8}$$

$$\sum_{k\in S}\sum_{i\in A}\sum_{j\in B} x_{ij}^k = \sum_{i\in A\cup B} p_i \tag{5.9}$$

In the above model, formula (5.4) indicates that the total travel time of passengers is the least. Equation (5.5) means that any car in the parking lot can only drive from any pick-up site in the area to any drop-off site in the drop-off area. Equation (5.6) indicates that the sum of the number of passengers at all stations cannot exceed the capacity of the vehicles providing services. Equation (5.7) means that any site can only be served by any vehicle. Equation (5.8) indicates that the number of passengers at any stop is less than the passenger capacity of the demand-responsive rural bus. Equation (5.9) represents the relationship between the number of passengers on the road segment and the number of passengers at the station. The meaning of each parameter in the formula is shown in Table 5.2.

Tab. 5.2　Symbol conventions

Symbol	Type	Convention
Z	parameter	Total travel time
S	parameter	Collection of vehicles
A	parameter	Collection of get-on station
B	parameter	Collection of get-off station
l_{ij}^{k}	parameter	Distance of bus k traveled from station i to station j
x_{ij}^{k}	variable	Bus k goes from stop i to stop j
q_{ij}^{k}	parameter	Number of passengers on bus k from station i to station j
p_i	parameter	Number of passengers at station i
t	parameter	Passenger's boarding time
y_{ik}	variable	Bus k serves station i
$k_{\max}$	parameter	Maximum number of vehicles participating in the service
Q	parameter	The passenger capacity of a vehicle

5.8　Genetic algorithm

Genetic algorithm is a search algorithm used to solve optimization in computational mathematics, and it is a kind of evolutionary algorithm. Evolutionary algorithms were originally developed based on some phenomena in evolutionary biology, including heredity, mutation, natural selection and hybridization. Genetic algorithm is usually implemented by computer simulation. For an optimization problem, a population of abstract representations of a given number of candidate solutions (called individuals) (called chromosomes) evolves toward a better solution. Traditionally, solutions are represented in binary (that is, strings of 0s and 1s), but other representations are possible. Evolution starts with a population of completely random individuals and then happens from generation to generation. In each generation, the fitness of the entire population is evaluated by randomly selecting multiple individuals (based on their fitness) from the current population to generate a new population of life through natural selection and mutation, which becomes the current population in the next iteration of the algorithm.

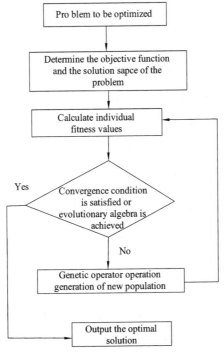

Fig. 5.4   Genetic algorithm

Figure 5.4 shows the overall idea of genetic algorithm. It can be seen from the figure that: for an optimization problem, the objective function should be determined according to the goal pursued, and the solution space of the problem should be determined at the same time. Then individual fitness value is calculated from the objective function, according to the fitness value to choose operation, thus for crossover operation and mutation operation, to generate new population, achieve convergence condition or the number of iterations when achieving the maximum number of iterations, get the optimal solution, otherwise, repeat the fitness value calculation, selection, crossover operation and mutation operation, etc.

5.8.1 Related concepts of genetic algorithm

1. Genes and chromosomes

In genetic algorithms, we first map the problem we are trying to solve to a mathematical problem, known as "mathematical modeling," where a viable solution to the problem is called a "chromosome." A viable solution generally consists of multiple elements, each of which is called a "gene" on a chromosome. For example, for equation (5.10), [1, 2, 3], [1, 3, 2] and [3, 2, 1] are feasible solutions of this function (i.e. feasible solutions when substituting), and these feasible solutions are all called chromosomes in the genetic algorithm.

$$3x + 4y + 5z < 100 \tag{5.10}$$

These feasible solutions are made up of three elements, so each element is called a gene that makes up a chromosome in genetic algorithms.

2. Encoding and decoding operations

Coding: The transformation of a feasible solution to a problem from its solution space to the search space of a genetic algorithm.

Decoding: Transformation of genetic algorithm solution space to problem space.

The commonly used encoding methods include binary encoding, gray encoding, floating point encoding, cascade encoding of each parameter, and cross encoding of each parameter, as follows:

(1) Binary coding method.

Disadvantages: there is a mapping error when the continuous function is discretized. It cannot directly reflect the structural characteristics of the problem being sought, and it is not convenient to develop genetic operators with specialized knowledge for the problem, and it is difficult to meet the building block coding principle.

(2) Gray code encoding: Only one code point is different between the codes corresponding to two consecutive integers, and the other code points are the same.

(3) Floating-point number coding method: Each gene value of an individual is represented by a certain floating-point number within a certain range, and the code length of the individual is equal to the number of bits of its decision variable.

(4) Each parameter cascade coding: a method of coding individuals with multiple variables. Usually, each parameter is coded by a certain coding method, and then their codes are connected in a certain order to form an individual code representing all the parameters.

(5) Multi-parameter cross-coding: The code points that play a

major role in each parameter are gathered together so that they are not easily destroyed by genetic operators.

Three norms for evaluating coding: completeness, soundness, and non-redundancy.

3. Fitness function

In nature, it seems, there exists a God who selects the better individuals of each generation and weeds out the less environmentally fit. So in genetic algorithms, how to measure the advantages and disadvantages of chromosomes? That's what the fitness function does. Fitness function plays this "god" role in genetic algorithm. The genetic algorithm will carry out N iterations during its operation, and each iteration will generate several chromosomes. Fitness function will give a score to all chromosomes generated in this iteration to judge the fitness of these chromosomes, and then eliminate the chromosomes with lower fitness and only retain the chromosomes with higher fitness, so that the quality of chromosomes will become better and better after several iterations. Fitness function, also known as evaluation function, is a standard to distinguish good or bad individuals in a group determined according to the objective function. The fitness function is always non-negative, while the objective function may be positive or negative, so it is necessary to transform between the objective function and the fitness function.

The general process of evaluating individual fitness is as follows:

① After decoding the individual coding string, the phenotype of the individual can be obtained.

② The value of the objective function can be calculated according to the phenotype of the individual.

③ According to the type of optimization problem, the individual fitness can be calculated from the value of the objective function according to certain transformation rules.

The design of fitness function should mainly meet the following requirements:

① Single-valued, continuous, non-negative, maximized.

② Reasonable and consistent.

③ Small amount of calculation.

④ Strong versatility.

The conversion method from objective function $F(x)$ to fitness function Fit(f(x)) is as follows: The objective function $F(x)$ to be solved directly is converted to fitness function.

Fit($f(x)$) = $f(x)$ is a maximization problem

Fit($f(x)$) = $-f(x)$ is a minimization problem

Fitness scaling: in different stages of genetic algorithm, the fitness of the individual is appropriately expanded or reduced. The commonly used scaling methods are as follows:

① Linear scaling: $F = af + b$

② Power scale transformation: $F = fk$

③ Exponential scaling: $F = \exp(-\text{beitaf})$

4. Select operation

The selection operation in the genetic algorithm is a kind of genetic operation used to determine how to select which individuals from the parent population in a certain way to pass on to the next population, to determine recombination or crossover individuals, and how many offspring individuals will be produced by the selected individuals. Commonly used selection operators:

① Roulette Wheel Selection is a kind of replay random sampling method. The probability of each individual going to the next generation is equal to the ratio of its fitness values to the fitness values of the entire population. The selection error is large.

② Stochastic Tournament: select a pair of individuals according to the roulette wheel each time, and then let the two individuals compete, the one with the highest fitness is selected, and so on until the selection is full.

③ Optimal reserved selection: firstly, the selection operation of genetic algorithm was carried out according to roulette selection method, and then the individual structure with the highest fitness in the current population was completely copied to the next generation population.

④ No replay random Selection (It is also called expected Value Selection) : Random Selection is performed according to the survival expectation of each individual in the next generation population. Methods the following:

Step1: Calculate the number N of survival expectations of each individual in the group in the next generation group.

Step2: If an individual is selected to participate in the crossover operation, then its expected survival in the next generation is subtracted by 0.5. If an individual is not selected to participate in the crossover operation, then its expected survival in the next generation is subtracted by 1.0.

Step3: As the selection process progresses, if an individual's expected survival number is less than 0, the individual will no longer have a chance to be selected.

① Deterministic selection: Perform selection operations in a deterministic way. The specific operation process is as follows:

Step1: Calculate the expected survival number N of each individual in the group in the next generation group.

Step2: Use the integer part of N to determine the survival number of each corresponding individual in the next generation group.

Step3: Use the decimal part of N to sort the individuals in descending order, and take the first M individuals in order to join the next generation group. So far, M individuals in the next generation can be completely determined.

② Random selection without replay remainder: It can ensure that some individuals with greater fitness than the average fitness can be inherited into the next generation population, so the selection error is relatively small.

③ Uniform sorting: Sort all the individuals in the group according to their period fitness, and assign the probability of each individual being selected based on this sorting.

④ The best preservation strategy: The most adaptive individual in the current population does not participate in the crossover and mutation operations, but instead uses it to replace the least adaptive individuals in the current generation group after crossover and mutation operations.

⑤ Random league selection: each time the individual with the highest fitness among several individuals is selected and inherited into the next generation population.

⑥ Exclusion selection: The newly generated offspring will replace or exclude the similar old parent individuals to increase the diversity of the group.

5. Crossover operation

The crossover operation of genetic algorithm refers to the exchange of some genes of two paired chromosomes in a certain way to form two new individuals. Simply understood as: each iteration of the genetic algorithm generates N chromosomes. In the genetic algorithm, each iteration is called an "evolution". So, how did the newly generated chromosomes come from each time? The answer is "crossover". The process of crossover needs to find two chromosomes from the chromosomes of the previous generation, one is the father and the other is the mother. Then a certain position of the two chromosomes is cut off and spliced together to generate a new chromosome. This new chromosome contains a certain number of father's genes as well as a certain number of mother's genes.

Crossover operators suitable for binary coded individuals or floating-point coded individuals:

① One-point Crossover: It means that only one crossover point is randomly set in the individual code string, and then part of the chromosomes of two paired individuals are exchanged at this point.

② Two-point crossing and multi-point crossing:

a. Two-point Crossover: Two crossover points are randomly set in the individual code string, and then partial gene exchange is performed.

b. Multi-point Crossover (Multi-point Crossover) randomly set multiple cross points in the individual code string, and then perform partial gene exchange.

③ Uniform Crossover (It is also called Uniform Crossover): The genes at each locus of two paired individuals are exchanged with the same crossover probability, thereby forming two new individuals.

④ Arithmetic Crossover: Two new individuals are produced by the linear combination of two individuals. The operation object is generally an individual represented by a floating-point number code.

6. Mutation operation

Crossover ensures that each evolution leaves a good gene, but it is merely a selection of the original result set, where the genes remain the same, but the order in which they are combined has been switched. This can only ensure that after N times of evolution, the calculation result is closer to the local optimal solution, but can never reach the global optimal solution. In order to solve this problem, we need to introduce variation.

Variation is easy to understand. When we generate a new chromosome through crossover, we need to randomly select several genes on the new chromosome, and then modify the value of genes randomly, so as to introduce new genes into the existing chromosome, which breaks through the current search restriction and is more conducive to the algorithm to find the global optimal solution.

Mutation operation in genetic algorithm refers to the replacement of gene values at some loci in the coding string of individual chromosome with other alleles at the loci, thus forming a new individual. The following mutation operators are applicable to binary and floating point encoding individuals:

① Basic bit mutation (Simple Mutation): Perform mutation operation on a certain bit or a few randomly designated digits in the individual code string with mutation probability and only due to the value of the seat.

② Uniform Mutation: Replace the original gene value at each locus in the individual coding string with a random number that meets the uniform distribution within a certain range with a certain small probability. (Especially it suitable for the primary operation stage of the algorithm)

③ Boundary Mutation: randomly select one of the two corresponding boundary gene values on the locus to replace the original gene value. It is especially suitable for a class of problems when the best point is at or close to the boundary of the feasible solution.

④ Non-uniform mutation: Make a random perturbation to the original gene value, and use the result of the perturbation as the new gene value after mutation. After the mutation operation is performed on each locus with the same probability, it is equivalent to a slight change of the entire solution vector in the solution space.

⑤ Gaussian approximate mutation: When performing mutation operation, replace the original gene value with a random number with the symbol mean value of P and the variance of the normal distribution of P_2.

7. Constraint processing

There are mainly the following methods for handling constraints:

① Search space limitation method: Limit the size of the search space of the genetic algorithm, so that there is a one-to-one correspondence between the point in the search space that represents an individual and the point in the solution space that represents a feasible solution.

② Feasible solution transformation method: In the transformation from individual genotype to individual phenotype, the process of making it meet the constraints is added, that is, to find the many-to-one transformation relationship between individual genotype and individual phenotype, which expands the search space. The individual produced in the evolution process can always be transformed into a feasible solution that satisfies the constraints in the outstanding space through this transformation.

③ Penalty function method: When calculating the fitness of an individual who has no corresponding feasible solution in the solution space, a penalty function is imposed to reduce the fitness of the individual and reduce the probability of the individual being inherited into the next generation population.

5.8.2 Characteristics of genetic algorithm

Genetic algorithm is a general algorithm for solving search problems, and it can be used for various general problems. The common features of search algorithms are:

(1) First form a set of candidate solutions.

(2) Calculate the fitness of these candidate solutions according to some adaptability conditions.

(3) Retain some candidate solutions according to fitness and discard other candidate solutions.

(4) Perform certain operations on the retained candidate solutions to generate new candidate solutions.

In the genetic algorithm, the above-mentioned features are combined in a special way: parallel search based on chromosome group, selection operation with guessing nature, exchange operation and mutation operation. This special combination method distinguishes genetic algorithm from other search algorithms. Genetic algorithm also has the following characteristics:

(1) Genetic algorithm searches from the string set of problem solutions, not from a single solution. This is a great difference between genetic algorithm and traditional optimization algorithm. Traditional optimization algorithms iteratively find the optimal solution from a single initial value; it is easy to stray into the local optimal solution. The genetic algorithm starts the search from the string set, and has a large coverage area, which is conducive to global selection.

(2) The genetic algorithm processes multiple individuals in the group at the same time, that is, evaluates multiple solutions in the search space, which reduces the risk of falling into a local optimal solution. At the same time, the algorithm itself is easy to parallelize.

(3) Genetic algorithms basically do not use search space knowledge or other auxiliary information, but only use fitness function values to evaluate individuals, and perform genetic operations on this basis. The fitness function is not only not restricted by continuous differentiability, but also its domain can be set arbitrarily. This feature greatly expands the application range of genetic algorithms.

(4) Genetic algorithm does not use deterministic rules, but uses probabilistic transition rules to guide its search direction.

(5) Self-organization, self-adaptation and self-learning. When the genetic algorithm uses the information obtained in the evolution process to organize the search by itself, individuals with greater fitness have a higher survival probability and obtain a genetic structure that is more adapted to the environment.

(6) In addition, the algorithm itself can also use dynamic adaptive technology to automatically adjust algorithm control parameters and coding accuracy during the evolution process, such as using fuzzy adaptive method.

5.8.3 The operation process of genetic algorithm

The genetic algorithm has a fixed basic process, which can be improved on the basis of the basic process according to different problems. The basic process is shown in Figure 5.5. It can be seen from the figure that the main operations of genetic algorithm include: encoding and decoding operations, fitness function value calculation, selection operations, crossover operations, mutation operations, and so on.

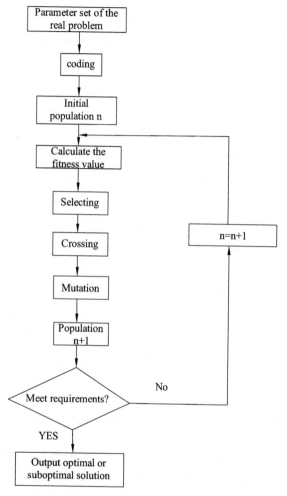

Fig. 5.5   Operation flow of genetic algorithm

The basic operation process of genetic algorithm is as follows:

Step1: Initialization: Set the evolution algebra counter $t=0$, set the maximum evolution algebra T, and randomly generate M individuals as the initial population $P(0)$.

Step2: Individual evaluation· calculate the fitness of each individual in population $P(t)$.

Step3: Selection operation: the selection operator is applied to the group. The purpose of selection is to pass optimized individuals directly to the next generation or to pass new individuals to the next generation through pairing and crossover. Selection is based on the fitness assessment of individuals in the population.

Step4: Crossover operation: the crossover operator is applied to the group. Crossover operator is the core of genetic algorithm.

Step5: Mutation operation: the mutation operator is applied to the population. That is to change the value of some loci on the individual string in the population.

The next generation population $P(t+1)$ is obtained after selection, crossover and mutation operation.

Step6: Judgment of termination condition: if $t = T$, the individual with the maximum fitness obtained in the evolution process is taken as the output of the optimal solution and the calculation is terminated.

5.8.4 Application of genetic algorithm

Genetic algorithm (GA) provides a general framework for solving complex system optimization problems. It is not dependent on the specific domain of the problem and has strong robustness to the types of problems. Therefore, it is widely used in many subjects. The following are some of the main applications of genetic algorithms.

1. Function optimization

Function optimization is a classical application field of genetic algorithm, and is also a common example to evaluate the performance of genetic algorithm. Many people have constructed a variety of complex forms of test functions. There are continuous functions and discrete functions, convex functions and concave functions, low-dimensional functions and high-dimensional functions, deterministic functions and random functions, single-peak functions and multi-peak functions. It is better to evaluate the performance of genetic algorithm by using these geometric functions with their own characteristics, but for some nonlinear, multi-model, multi-objective function optimization problems, it is difficult to solve by other optimization methods. But genetic algorithm can get better result easily.

2. Combination optimization

With the increase of the problem size, the search space of combinatorial optimization problem also expands sharply. Sometimes it is difficult or even impossible to find the exact optimal solution by enumeration method on current computers. For this kind of complex problem, people have realized that we should focus on finding the satisfactory solution, and genetic algorithm is one of the best tools to find the satisfactory solution. Practice has proved that genetic algorithm has been successfully applied to solve NP difficulty problems such as traveling salesman problem, backpack problem, packing problem, layout optimization, graph partition problem and so on.

3. Production scheduling problems

In many cases, the mathematical model of production scheduling problems is difficult to be solved accurately, even if it can be solved after some simplification. It also simplifies so much that the result is far from the actual result. At present, the actual production is mainly based on some experience to carry out scheduling. Genetic algorithm has become an effective tool for solving complex scheduling problems. Genetic algorithm has been applied effectively in the scheduling of single production shop, production line, production planning, task assignment and so on.

4. Automatic control

There are many optimization related problems to be solved in the field of automatic control. Genetic algorithm (GA) has been applied preliminarily and has shown good results. For example, using the genetic algorithm optimization of the control system of aviation, space and use genetic algorithm to design controller, fuzzy controller based on genetic algorithm optimization design, parameter identification based on genetic algorithm, fuzzy control rules based on genetic algorithm learning, using the genetic algorithm of artificial neural network structure optimization design and weights of learning, etc. It shows the possibility of applying genetic algorithm in this field.

5. Robotics

Robot is a kind of complex artificial system which is difficult to model accurately, and the origin of genetic algorithm comes from the research of artificial adaptive system. Therefore, robotics has naturally become an important application area of genetic algorithms. For example, genetic algorithm has been studied and applied in mobile robot path planning, joint robot trajectory planning, robot inverse kinematics solution, cell robot structure optimization and behavior coordination, etc.

6. Image processing

Image processing is an important research field in computer vision. In the process of image processing, such as scanning, feature extraction, image segmentation, there will inevitably be some errors, which affect the image effect. How to minimize these errors is an important requirement to make computer vision practical. Genetic algorithm has found its application in the optimization calculation of these image processing. At present, it has been applied in pattern recognition (including Chinese character recognition), image restoration, image edge feature extraction and so on.

7. Artificial life

Human life is a man-made system with unique behavior of natural biological system, which is simulated or constructed by computer, machine and other human media. Self-organizing ability and self-learning ability are two main characteristics of human life. There is a close relationship between human life and genetic algorithm. Evolution model based on genetic algorithm is an important basic theory to study the phenomenon of human life. Although the research of human life is still in the enlightenment stage, genetic algorithm has shown its preliminary application ability in its evolution model, learning model, behavior model, self-organization model and so on, and which will get more in-depth application and development. Artificial life and genetic algorithm complement each other. Genetic algorithm provides an effective tool for the research of human life, and the research of human life will promote the further development of genetic algorithm.

8. Genetic programming

In 1989, Professor Koza of Standford University developed the concept of genetic programming, which is based on the idea of using tree structure to express computer programs, using the idea of genetic algorithm, through the automatic generation of computer programs to solve problems. Although the theory of genetic programming is still young and its application is limited, it has been successfully applied to artificial intelligence, machine learning and other fields. At present, there are more than ten experimental genetic programming systems in public. For example, ADF system developed by Koza, GPELST system developed by While, etc.

9. Machine learning

Learning ability is one of the abilities of advanced adaptive systems. Machine learning based on genetic algorithm, especially classifier system, has been applied in many fields. For example, genetic algorithm is used to learn fuzzy control rules, and genetic algorithm is used to learn membership function, so as to better improve the performance of fuzzy system. Machine learning based on genetic algorithm can be used to adjust the connection weight of artificial neural network, and can also be used to optimize the structure of artificial neural network. The classifier system has also been successfully applied in the path planning system of learning multi-robots.

10. Data mining

Data mining is a database technology emerging in recent years. It can extract hidden, previously unknown and potentially valuable knowledge and rules from large databases. Many data mining problems can be regarded as search problems, database as search space, mining algorithm as search strategy. Therefore, genetic algorithms are applied to search the database to evolve a randomly generated set of rules. Until the database can be overridden by the set of rules, thus mining the rules hidden in the database. Sunil has successfully developed a data mining tool based on genetic algorithm. The results show that genetic algorithm is one of the effective methods for data mining.

5.9 Chapter summary

This chapter introduces the configuration of rural passenger transport capacity. First, it introduces the mode of rural passenger transport capacity, and then introduces the influencing factors of rural passenger transport capacity. It is believed that the influencing factors include the total capacity and the structure of transport capacity, and each category is detailed. analyze. Secondly, it introduces the model configuration of rural passenger transport, including configuration ideas, configuration principles, etc. Then it introduces the general principles of capacity allocation and the basic steps of capacity allocation. Finally, the conventional operation of rural passenger transportation capacity configuration is introduced, and on this basis, the capacity configuration method of demand-responsive rural public transport is studied, the capacity configuration route optimization model is constructed, and the genetic algorithm for solving the model is introduced.

5.10 References

[1] Dai Tongyan, Sun Xueqin. Transportation histology [M]. Beijing: China Machine Press, 2006.

[2] Li Hongxia. Research on rural passenger line network planning of Langfang [D]. Tianjin: Hebei University of Technology, 2008.

[3] Wu Qiang, Liu Xu. Research on rural passenger transport capacity investment strategy [D]. Chengdu: Southwest Jiaotong University, 2008.

[4] Luo Qingyu. Research on bidding problem of road passenger line management right [J]. Integrated Transportation, 2003(1): 54-55.

[5] Li Bo. Study on rural passenger transport capacity allocation in western mountainous area [D]. Chongqing: Chongqing Jiaotong University, 2013.

[6] Song Cui. Study on development planning of urban and rural public passenger transport at county level [D]. Xi'an: Chang'an University, 2011.

Chapter 6

Case study on demand-responsive rural passenger transport capacity in the Hui autonomous prefecture of Linxia

6.1 Background

This book takes the Hui autonomous prefecture of Linxia as the research scope. Linxia Hui Autonomous Prefecture, formerly known as Hezhou, is an Autonomous Prefecture under the jurisdiction of Gansu Province, one of the two Hui autonomous prefectures in China and one of the two ethnic autonomous prefectures in Gansu Province. It was established in November 1956. As of April 2021, the total area of the state was 8169 square kilometers, There are 42 ethnic groups in the prefecture, including Hui, Han, Dongxiang, Baoan and Sala.

Dongxiang and Baoan are unique ethnic minorities in Gansu with Linxia as the main residential area.

Linxia is located in Western China, in the southwest of central Gansu Province and in the upper reaches of the Yellow River. It is the hub of the South Road of the ancient Silk Road, the important town of the Tang fan ancient road and the center of tea horse exchange.

6.2 Data collection

Taking a certain area of Linxia Prefecture as the study area, it is planned to collect the rural passenger transport demand in peak hours of each day in the whole year. Due to the limited data sources and research time, this paper only collects the rural passenger transport demand in peak hours of each day in the whole study area in a week, and its passenger transport demand is shown in Table 6.1.

Table 6.1　Daily peak hour passenger demand in a week

Time	Passenger demand in peak hours (person/h)
Monday	500
Tuesday	550
Wednesday	560
Thursday	520
Friday	590
Saturday	650
Sunday	680

It can be seen from Table 6.1 that the minimum passenger demand in peak hours of each day in this week is 500 people / h and the maximum is 680 people/h. Since it is necessary to obtain the number of conventionally equipped vehicles of demand responsive rural public transport, it is necessary to consider the maximum number of vehicles required in this area under the limit state, 680 is taken as the passenger demand in peak hours in all days of the year. Firstly, according to the calculation formula of the overall transport capacity scale of an area in Linxia Prefecture in section 5.6.1, the overall transport capacity scale of an area in Linxia Prefecture is calculated. The values of the parameters in the formula are as follows: the average transport distance of rural passenger transport in the area is 10km, the average directional non-uniformity coefficient of passenger flow in the area is 1.2, the seasonal non-uniformity coefficient of passenger flow in the area is 3, and the number of lines in peak hours is 10, The peak hour operation speed is 20km/h, the peak hour operation speed correction coefficient is 0.8, and the average full load coefficient of vehicles in peak hours is 0.75. The values of various parameters are selected according to the actual situation of each region. By substituting the values of various parameters into the formula in section 5.6.1, we can get:

$$Q_z = \frac{680 \times 10 \times 1.2 \times 3}{10 \times 20 \times 0.8 \times 0.75}$$

$$Q_z = 204$$

According to the above formula, each line in the area can serve 204 people in peak hours, and there are 10 lines in the whole area in peak hours, which can serve 2040 people in total. Therefore, the capacity scale of the whole area in peak hours is 2040 people/hour.

Secondly, the calculation formula of line capacity allocation in section 5.6.2 is used to calculate the line capacity in this area. Since the departure frequency is involved in the line capacity allocation formula, the departure frequency is calculated first. The values of various parameters are: the maximum passenger flow of the line in peak hours is 32 people/hour, and the average full load coefficient of vehicles in peak hours is 0.75. Because the models selected in this paper are divided into large, medium and small. There are three small models, and the passenger capacity of each model is different. The medium-sized vehicle is selected this time, so the passenger capacity of the vehicle is 15people/vehicle, so we can get:

$$n = \frac{32}{0.75 \times 15} \approx 3$$

Namely the departure interval is 3 h. In order to solve the maximum number of vehicles required for peak hours of a single line, the parameter values are set as follows: the line length is 10km, the vehicle operation speed is 20 km/h, and the stop time of one-way station is 0.05 h. Substitute the parameter values into the formula to obtain:

$$W = 2 \times \left(\frac{10}{20} + 0.05 \right) \times 3 = 3.3$$

Namely the maximum number of vehicles required for a single line in peak hours is 4. From the above calculation of capacity allocation, firstly, the number of passengers that can be transported in peak hours of each line can be calculated according to the maximum rural passenger transport demand in peak hours every day in a week, so as to estimate the overall capacity allocation scale of an area; Secondly, according to the specific peak hour passenger demand of each line, the departure frequency of each line in peak hours can be solved, so as to estimate the maximum number of vehicles required for a single line in peak hours.

Whether the estimated overall transport capacity of the area or the maximum number of vehicles required for a single line in peak hours is only to estimate the maximum number of demand responsive rural public transport that should be reserved in the area under normal circumstances. The reality is that the daily rural passenger transport volume of an area changes dynamically and has strong randomness. At the same time, Passengers are scattered in various villages and towns, and the number of passengers, travel time and travel location are unknown. If the line and departure time are fixed, it can be more acceptable to passengers to a certain extent, but it may cause a great waste of vehicle resources. Therefore, it is impossible to formulate a fixed line and team plan according to the conventional method. It is necessary to introduce demand responsive rural public transport service, which can solve the problem of travel convenience of rural residents on the one hand, and make full use of vehicle resources on the other hand.

Demand responsive rural public transport service has its special characteristics. The formulation of its operation lines needs to be completed before departure. Therefore, passengers need to make an appointment one day in advance, whether by telephone or mobile app. After receiving the passenger travel reservation information, the regional bus company processes the information and feeds back the processing results to the passengers in a reasonable form, so that the passengers can calmly arrange the travel plan. One day, the area receives a certain number of passenger travel information. After processing, the information is shown in table 6.2.

Table 6.2   Passenger information

Boarding station number	Number of passengers	Alighting station number	Number of passengers
1	10	14	8
2	8	15	18
3	13	16	12
4	18	17	13
5	16	18	20
6	7	19	16
7	14	20	10
8	20	21	7
9	9	22	6
10	12	23	20
11	20	24	14
12	6	25	13
13	13	26	9

It can be seen from table 6.2 that a total of 166 people in the area have travel needs one day. These passengers are scattered in different places, and their destinations are also distributed in different places. After systematic processing, 13 temporary boarding points and 13 temporary alighting points are formed. According to the principle of proximity, passengers need to get on at the nearest boarding point for subsequent processing, Number these boarding stations as 1, 2, 3, 4, 5, 6, 7, 8, 9, 10, 11, 12 and 13, and the lower station points as 14, 15, 16, 17, 18, 19, 20, 21, 22, 23, 24, 25 and 26. The number of passengers at each station has been fixed, and passengers from different boarding stations go to different alighting stations.

Different regions use different models for service. In this paper, there are three models, including large, medium and small models. Among them, the large-scale on-board passenger capacity is 20, the medium-sized on-board passenger capacity is 15 and the small on-board passenger capacity is 7. Due to the complexity of mixing and matching of different models, this example only considers the service of one model, and the matching service of different models will be left in the follow-up study. The calculation example adopts a large vehicle with a passenger capacity of 20 people.

There is only one demand responsive rural bus parking lot in this area, numbered a. for the distance between the parking lot and each up and down station point can be see in table 6.3. The value of each parameter is: person/vehicle, km/h, min. The genetic algorithm designed in section 5.8 is used to solve the demand responsive rural passenger bus capacity allocation line optimization model. Based on the code block platform, C++ code is written to realize the solution algorithm. The parameters are set as follows: the population size is 100, the maximum number of iterations is 100, the segment crossover probability is 0.8, and the segment mutation probability is 0.1. After running the program for many times, the optimal solution of the problem is obtained.

Table 6.3 Node spacing (unit: km)

distance	a	1	2	3	4	5	6	7	8	9	10	11	12	13	14	15	16	17	18	19	20	21	22	23	24	25	26
a	0	5	6.3	7.6	12	11	10	13	6	15	14	17	8	7	13	11	9	8	16	11	14	10	7	4.5	8.8	5.5	7.8
1	5	0	4.8	5.6	4.8	6.9	5.5	6.9	8.8	7.8	5.8	6.9	7.5	8.9	5.7	15	8.9	7.8	9.9	7.6	6.8	5.8	6.9	7.8	6.8	8.5	7.8
2	6.3	4.8	0	8	12	15	13	7	6	23	12	7	9	11	12	10	11	6	8	15	11	10	8	11	13	8	6
3	7.6	5.6	8	0	5.6	6.9	7.1	8	10	12	8.9	7.7	6.6	8.9	8.2	6.9	5.7	14	10	8	7	9	11	8.9	7.9	8.9	5.4
4	12	4.8	12	5.6	0	10	11	9	7	5	6	7	9	10	11	8	5	8	9	14	13	12	11	16	10	14	11
5	11	6.9	15	6.9	10	0	10	6	7	8	8	9	10	15	7	6	10	18	11	6	7	8	9	14	6	8	15
6	10	5.5	13	7.1	11	10	0	5	4	3	8	6	16	11	12	17	10	9	8	7	6	12	10	9	8	7	6
7	13	6.9	7	8	9	6	5	0	9	7	8	6	7	8	6	7	9	8	11	10	6	7	8	13	13	15	9
8	6	8.8	6	10	7	7	4	9	0	14	16	10	8	9	6	11	8	10	8	9	10	8	8	9	10	14	10
9	15	7.8	23	12	5	8	3	7	14	0	9	8	10	8	9	8	7	9	7	9	8	6	7	9	11	14	13
10	14	5.8	12	8.9	6	8	8	8	16	9	0	11	9	7	9	8	10	14	9	10	14	9	8	8	7	9	14
11	17	6.9	7	7.7	7	9	6	6	10	8	11	0	2	5	4	6	7	9	10	8	9	14	8	9	10	9	15
12	8	7.5	9	6.6	9	10	16	7	8	10	9	2	0	9	8	7	6	7	9	12	6	8	10	6	5	8	9
13	7	8.9	11	8.9	10	15	11	8	9	8	7	5	9	0	5	6	7	9	8	4	6	7	8	10	6	9	10

续表

distance	a	1	2	3	4	5	6	7	8	9	10	11	12	13	14	15	16	17	18	19	20	21	22	23	24	25	26
14	13	5.7	12	8.2	11	7	12	6	6	9	9	4	8	5	0	8	9	16	7	9	6	12	6	8	9	13	6
15	11	15	10	6.9	8	6	17	7	11	8	8	6	7	6	8	0	6	9	10	9	8	13	8	9	10	11	8
16	9	8.9	11	5.7	5	10	10	9	8	7	10	7	6	7	9	6	0	9	10	8	7	6	8	5	9	7	10
17	8	7.8	6	14	8	18	9	8	10	9	14	9	7	9	16	9	9	0	9	10	9	7	6	8	9	10	14
18	16	9.9	8	10	9	11	8	11	8	7	9	10	9	8	7	10	10	9	0	6	9	7	8	6	10	9	12
19	11	7.6	15	8	14	6	7	10	9	9	10	8	12	4	9	9	8	10	6	0	12	6	9	7	9	10	4
20	14	6.8	11	7	13	7	6	6	10	8	14	9	6	6	6	8	7	9	9	12	0	9	10	6	10	9	14
21	10	5.8	10	9	12	8	12	7	8	6	9	14	8	7	12	13	6	7	7	6	9	0	9	11	9	8	7
22	7	6.9	8	11	11	9	10	8	8	7	8	8	10	8	6	8	8	6	8	9	10	9	0	9	8	12	14
23	4.5	7.8	11	8.9	16	14	9	13	9	9	7	9	6	10	8	9	5	8	6	7	6	11	9	0	8	7	9
24	8.8	6.8	13	7.9	10	6	8	13	10	11	9	10	5	6	9	10	9	9	10	9	10	9	8	8	0	9	10
25	5.5	8.5	8	6.8	14	8	7	15	14	14	14	9	8	9	13	11	7	10	9	10	9	8	12	7	9	0	8
26	7.8	7.8	6	5.4	11	15	6	9	10	13	14	15	9	10	6	8	10	14	12	4	14	7	14	9	10	8	0

After running this program for many times, a total of five optimization results are obtained. The same point is that the target values of the five optimization results are the same, which are 80.3238 h. The difference is that the five optimization schemes are different and the vehicle driving routes are different. Tables 6.4, 6.5, 6.6, 6.7 and 6.8 are presented to clarify which scheme is the best. For convenience, tables 6.4, 6.5, 6.6, 6.7 and 6.8 are named as scheme1, scheme2, scheme3, scheme4 and scheme5.

Table 6.4   Scheme1

Chromosome	a 12 9 13 3 6 11 5 1 2 4 7 10 8 16 22 14 24 20 26 25 21 23 18 15 17 19		
Vehicle number	Route site	Number of passengers	Occupancy rate (%)
1	12—9—22—26	15	75
2	13—17	13	65
3	3—6—25—21	20	100
4	11—18	20	100
5	5—19	16	80
6	1—2—14—20	18	90
7	4—15	18	90
8	7—24	14	70
9	10—16	12	60
10	8—23	20	100

It can be seen from table 6.4 that a total of 10 demand responsive rural public buses are required to participate in the service in this scheme. The stations required by each vehicle are known, the number of passengers required to be served is known, the passenger seating rate of each vehicle is known, and the passenger seating rate of all vehicles has reached more than 60%, of which the passenger seating rate of vehicle 3, vehicle 4 and vehicle 10 has reached 100%, it indicates that there are no seats left in the vehicle. On the whole, the occupancy rate of all vehicles remains at a high level, and there is no low passenger occupancy rate. Locally, the passenger occupancy rate of several vehicles remains high, indicating that this route optimization scheme has great advantages in passenger occupancy rate. The average occupancy rate of vehicles is 83%.

Table 6.5   Scheme2

Chromosome	a 9 6 2 4 13 7 11 1 10 5 12 8 3 19 25 18 15 22 26 20 17 21 14 16 23 24		
Vehicle number	Route site	Number of passengers	Occupancy rate (%)
1	9—6—26—21	16	80
2	2—14	8	40
3	4—15	18	90
4	13—17	13	65
5	7—24	14	70
6	11—18	20	100
7	1—20	10	50
8	10—16	12	60
9	5—19	16	80
10	12—22	6	30
11	8—23	20	100
12	3—25	13	65

It can be seen from table 6.5 that a total of 12 demand responsive rural buses are required to participate in the service in this scheme. The stations required by each rural bus are known, the number of passengers required by each vehicle is known, and the passenger seating rate of each vehicle is known. The passenger occupancy rate in this scheme shows a polarization trend. In terms of high passenger occupancy rate, the passenger occupancy rate of 5 vehicles is more than 80%, of which the passenger occupancy rate of 2 vehicles is as high as 100%. In terms of low passenger occupancy rate, the passenger occupancy rate of 3 vehicles is less than 50%. Overall, the occupancy rate of passengers in this scheme is not very ideal. The average occupancy rate of vehicles is 69.16%.

Table 6.6   Scheme3

Chromosome	a 1 12 10 9 7 11 2 4 8 5 13 3 6 16 17 14 24 26 18 15 20 23 19 22 21 25		
Vehicle number	Route site	Number of passengers	Occupancy rate (%)
1	1—12—20—22	16	80
2	10—16	12	60
3	9—26	9	45
4	7—24	14	70
5	11—18	20	100
6	2—14	8	40
7	4—15	18	90
8	8—23	20	100
9	5—19	16	80
10	13—17	13	65
11	3—6—21—25	20	100

It can be seen from Table 6.6 that a total of 11 demand responsive rural buses are required to participate in the service in this scheme. The stations required by each vehicle are known, the number of passengers required by each vehicle is known, and the passenger occupancy rate of each vehicle is known. In this scheme, the passenger occupancy rate of three vehicles is as high as 100%, which are vehicle 5, vehicle 8 and vehicle 11 respectively, and the passenger occupancy rate of two vehicles is less than 50%, which are vehicle 3 and vehicle 6 respectively. The passenger occupancy rate of other vehicles is between 60% and 90%. The average occupancy rate of vehicles is 75.45%.

Table 6.7   Scheme4

Chromosome	a 5 11 2 6 9 10 1 8 7 4 13 12 3 16 17 18 26 21 14 25 15 23 22 19 20 24		
Vehicle number	Route site	Number of passengers	Occupancy rate (%)
1	5—19	16	80
2	11—18	20	100
3	2—6—21—14	15	75
4	9—26	9	45
5	10—16	12	60
6	1—20	10	50
7	8—23	20	100
8	7—24	14	70
9	4—15	18	90
10	13—12—17—22	19	95
11	3—25	13	65

It can be seen from Table 6.7 that there are 11 demand responsive rural public transports participating in the service in this scheme. The station required by each vehicle is known, the number of passengers required by each vehicle is known, and the passenger occupancy rate of each vehicle is known. In terms of high passenger occupancy rate, the passenger occupancy rate of vehicle 2 and vehicle 7 is as high as 100%. In terms of low passenger occupancy rate, the passenger occupancy rate of two vehicles is less than 60%, which are vehicle 4 and vehicle 6 respectively. The occupancy rate of other vehicles is between 60% and 90%. The average occupancy rate of vehicles is 75.45%.

Table 6.8   Scheme5

Chromosome	a 5 4 7 9 13 10 3 1 2 12 6 11 8 26 25 22 17 19 15 24 23 20 21 14 18 16		
Vehicle number	Route site	Number of passengers	Occupancy rate(%)
1	5—19	16	80
2	4—15	18	90
3	7—24	14	70
4	9—26	9	45
5	13—17	13	65
6	10—16	12	60
7	3—25	13	65
8	1—2—20—14	18	90
9	12—6—22—21	13	65
10	11—18	20	100
11	8—23	20	100

It can be seen from table 6.8 that this scheme requires 11 demand responsive rural public transports to participate in the service. The station required by each vehicle is known, the number of passengers required by each vehicle is known, and the passenger seating rate of each vehicle is known. In terms of high passenger seating rate, the passenger seating rate of 4 vehicles is more than 90%, of which the passenger seating rate of vehicle 10 and vehicle 11 is as high as 100%, The passenger occupancy rate of vehicle 2 and vehicle 8 is 90%. In terms of low passenger seating rate, only vehicle 4 has a passenger seating rate of less than 60%. The passenger occupancy rate of other vehicles is between 60% and 90%. The average occupancy rate of vehicles is 75.45%.

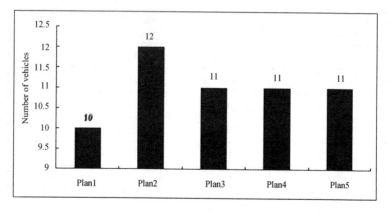

Figure 6.1   comparison of the number of vehicles in each scheme

Figure 6.1 shows the comparison of the number of vehicles required for each alternative. It can be seen from the figure that the minimum number of vehicles required for scheme 1 is 10, the maximum number of vehicles required for scheme 2 is 12, and the number of vehicles required for schemes 3, 4 and 5 is 11. Since the optimization target values obtained by the five schemes are the same and the number of passengers served by the five schemes is the same, it is natural to want to get as few vehicles as possible to participate in the service on the premise of meeting the travel needs of passengers and completing the same passenger transport task. Therefore, scheme 1 is the best scheme, The bus company only needs to send 10 demand responsive rural buses to complete the passenger transport task on that day.

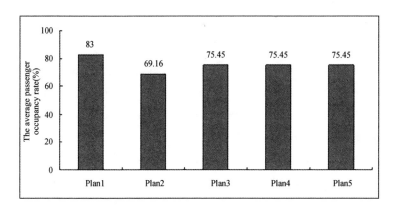

Figure 6.2   comparison of average passenger occupancy rate of each scheme

Figure 6.2 shows the comparison of the average passenger seating rate of each scheme. It can be seen from the figure that the average passenger seating rate of scheme 1 is the highest, which is 83%, the average passenger seating rate of scheme 2 is the lowest, which is 69.16%, and the average passenger seating rate of schemes 3, 4 and 5 is 75.45%. It shows that in terms of average passenger occupancy rate, scheme 2 is the worst, scheme 3, scheme 4 and scheme 5 are in the middle, and scheme 1 is the best.

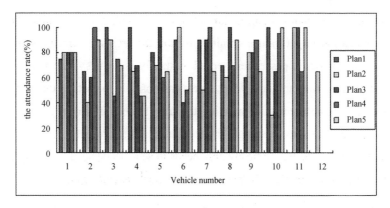

Figure 6.3   comparison of passenger occupancy rate of each vehicle in each scheme

Figure 6.3 shows the comparison of passenger occupancy rate of vehicles in each scheme. It can be seen from the figure that the red indicates the passenger occupancy rate of vehicles in scheme 1. The passenger occupancy rate of vehicles in scheme 1 is higher than 60%, while the occupancy rate of vehicles in schemes 2, 3, 4 and 5 is lower than 60%. It shows that selecting scheme 1 as the optimal scheme can not only complete the passenger transport task, And the number of vehicles used is less than other schemes. At the same time, whether from the macro level or micro level, the passenger seating rate of vehicles in scheme 1 is better than other schemes, so scheme 1 is the best scheme.

6.3   Summary

This chapter is an example application. Firstly, the background of the example is introduced. This example selects a region of Northwest

Linxia Hui Autonomous Prefecture as the background. Secondly, the general situation of the calculation example is introduced in detail, including the calculation of regional capacity allocation scale and the estimation of single line capacity allocation. At the same time, the genetic algorithm is programmed to solve the line optimization scheme in the capacity allocation, and the alternative schemes are compared and analyzed to determine the final optimization scheme.

6.4 References

[1] An Tong. Research on urban customized bus operation system and route design[D]. Changsha University of technology, 2016.

[2] Qiu Guo. Research on optimization method of customized bus line design based on passenger travel mode selection[D]. Beijing Jiaotong University, 2019.

[3] Zhang Hangqi. Research on customized bus route planning based on granular computing[D]. Hangzhou University of Electronic Science and technology, 2019.

[4] Gao Yan. Research on route planning of rural passenger vehicles concurrently engaged in express distribution[D]. Beijing Jiaotong University, 2020.

[5] Cao Liufang. Optimization of urban and rural customized bus lines in rural areas with weak passenger flow[D]. Hefei University of technology, 2019.

[6] Chen Xingying. Customized bus line generation and operation optimization under random user demand[D]. Chang'an University, 2019.

[7] Xu Rongrong. Research on the application of demand responsive public transport in rural passenger transport[D]. Chang'an University, 2015.

[8] Wang Jiao. Research on customized bus stop planning and timetable preparation[D]. Beijing Jiaotong University, 2016.

[9] Wu Zhenyu. Optimization of urban customized bus network for commuter demand[D]. Hefei University of technology, 2017.

Chapter 7

Demand-responsive routing optimization model and algorithm for rural passenger vehicles

7.1 Research background

At present, there are few studies on the optimization of demand-responsive bus routes in rural areas, but there are also a lot of analyses and answers to the problems of rural passenger transport and studies on the route optimization of related customized bus/coach. Lei et al. [1] analyzed and studied the current situation of rural passenger transport development and pointed out the shortage of transport capacity. Lu [2] optimized the rural passenger transport system under low-carbon economy by optimizing the layout of rural passenger transport network and hub stations. Hu [3] established the urban-rural integrated transportation organization framework through trunk and branch line planning method and passenger transportation forecast. An[4] used AP clustering algorithm, designed a bi-level constraint programming model, and used simulated annealing algorithm to optimize the layout of shared stations. Zhang [5] and others established a traffic compactness model to optimize the rural highway passenger transport lines. Zhang [6] established a multi-objective model with the objective function of maximum bus coverage, highest average attendance rate and minimum total investment in bus operation, and obtained excellent route optimization results by using ant colony algorithm. Qiu[7] established a bi-level programming model based on the results of passengers' travel mode selection, solved the upper-level model with branch and bound algorithm, and solved the lower-level model with improved allocation algorithm combining Dial algorithm with successive average algorithm (MSA). Shen [8] established the objective function with the minimum total cost based on the shortest reliability path, and adopted the emergency algorithm to get more reliable results than the shortest route scheme. Zhang [9] obtained three customized bus routes by using improved AP clustering and ant colony algorithm based on granular computing methodology. Tao[10] and others used the improved NSGA-II algorithm to solve the multi-objective model, which can meet the requirements of short passenger travel time and low vehicle fuel consumption. Gao [11] established the fixed route planning and variable route model of rural passenger vehicles which also engaged in express delivery, and solved them by tabu search algorithm, and worked out the scale and route scheme of rural passenger vehicles. Cao [12] used genetic algorithm to optimize the on-board passenger flow model, the off-board passenger flow model and the customized bus scheduling model based on OD demand. Chen [13] used the main objective method to solve the route planning and operation optimization model established by the mechanism in three cases of whether the starting and ending points of customized bus are fixed or not, and obtained the result that customized bus can greatly reduce travel expenses on the basis of increasing travel time. Wang et al. [14] solved the emergency customized bus route optimization model under public health emergencies by combining genetic algorithm and greedy algorithm, and obtained the route optimization scheme of customized bus under emergency scenes. The research of Xu [15] on demand-responsive public transport in rural areas proved that demand-responsive public transport in rural areas can effectively utilize vehicle resources and reduce operating costs. Wang[16] constructed the model of simultaneous optimization of timetable, station and route based on commuter travel demand data, and taking the number of vehicles, station number and departure time as decision variables, and he designed the corresponding solution algorithm, which provided a new idea for customized bus route planning. Wu[17] established path planning models for the boarding and alighting areas of passenger flow (the boarding area path model is the lowest total cost and the alighting area path model is the shortest travel time), which provided a new model for the commuter travel path planning method. To sum up, more in-depth research is needed on the route optimization of demand-responsive public transport in rural areas. In this paper, the improved genetic algorithm is used to solve the route optimization of public transport in rural areas.

7.2   Modeling of Rural Passenger Transport

7.2.1   Problem description

There are several pick-up and drop-off stations in rural areas and several passenger stations in urban areas. Each station in rural areas can only be served by a customized bus and can only be served once during each operation. Moreover, each bus has the same model and the same nuclear capacity, which can serve multiple stations, however, the number of passengers cannot exceed the nuclear capacity. The problem that needs to be solved is to minimize the cost of the bus company on the premise of meeting the demand of passengers. The schematic diagram of vehicle service path is shown in Figure 7.1, among which, the service process of demand-responsive bus in rural areas is as follows: after passengers inputting their own ride information into the mini program of Village-to-Village Communication for Rural Passenger Transport, the bus departs from a certain passenger station during the day according to the demand of passengers, and goes to the boarding station in the rural boarding area to receive passengers until it reaches the nuclear load limit, and it returns to the originally departed passenger station after serving the last passenger who gets off to pick up all the customers who want to enter the city. Similarly, the customers staying in the city during the day want to go home at night, they also need to enter their ride information into the mini program of Rural Passenger Transport Village to Village and then arrive at the passenger station at the specified time and take the passenger bus. The bus will return the passengers to the drop-off station to be reached according to the prescribed route in turn and finally return to the original passenger station (i.e., the station in the rural area is the passenger boarding station during the day and the drop-off station at night).

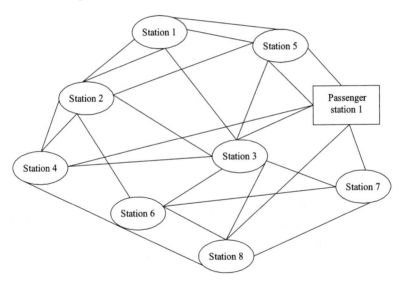

Fig.7.1　Schematic diagram of vehicle service route

7.2.2 Model assumptions

According to the situation of transporting passengers in rural areas, some simplifications are made to the model, and the following assumptions are set.

(1) There are the number of buses at the passenger station that can meet the demand of all passengers in the road network, and each passenger car has the same model and the same approved capacity.

(2) Each site can only be served once.

(3) Each bus can serve multiple stations.

(4) The number of passengers on & off stations has been determined, and the total number of passengers on each station will not exceed the approved capacity of a single passenger car.

(5) The distance between different nodes is known.

7.2.3 Symbol definition of model

Tab. 7.1   Symbol definition

Symbol	The definition of the symbol or related factors	Type
S_0	Set of "Rural Passenger Transport Village to Village" passenger station in cities and towns. $S_0 = \{s \mid s = 1, 2, \cdots, S\}$	Set
I	Set of demand sites in rural areas $I = \{i \mid i = 1, 2, \cdots, m\}$	Set
d_{ijr}^s	The distance from the station i to j of the r bus at the s passenger terminal, the unit is km	Parameter
p_i	The number of people at the i getting on or off station	Parameter
K	Represents the operating vehicle that carries passengers on the road network	Parameter
f_0	Fuel cost per kilometer for passenger buses	Parameter
f_0'	Other fixed costs per passenger buses	Parameter
Q_{pr}	The number of passengers on vehicle r on route p	Parameter

Symbol	The definition of the symbol or related factors	Type
A_{pr}	Attendance in route p	Parameter
$a_{\min}$	Minimum attendance in the route	Parameter
C	The number of authorized passengers of the passenger buses	Parameter
x_{ijr}^s	$x_{ijr}^s = 1$, The r bus in the s parking lot travels from station i to j. $x_{ijr}^s = 0$, otherwise.	Variable
Q	The total number of passengers who need to ride on the route	Variable
R	Number of buses operated	Variable

7.2.4 Objective function

With the goal of minimizing the total operating cost, the objective function formula (7.1) is established, in which fuel costs account for the main cost.

$$
\begin{aligned}
f = \min\{f_0[&\sum_{s \in S_0} \sum_{r \in p_s} \sum_{i \in S_0} \sum_{j \in I} d_{ijr}^s x_{ijr}^s + \\
&\sum_{s \in S_0} \sum_{r \in p_s} \sum_{i \in I} \sum_{j \in I} d_{ijr}^s x_{ijr}^s + \\
&\sum_{s \in S_0} \sum_{r \in p_s} \sum_{i \in I} \sum_{j \in S_0} d_{ijr}^s x_{ijr}^s] + Rf_0'
\end{aligned}
\tag{7.1}
$$

7.2.5 Constraints

1. vehicle capacity constraints (supply and demand constraints)

There is an upper limit on the number of passengers on board the rural "village-to-village" buses, which should not exceed the number of passengers on board when the vehicles are running. At the same time, all passengers start in advance by collecting demand, i.e., the total demand in the road network cannot exceed the total supply provided by the vehicles to be started in all parking lots, so there are the following constraints.

$$\sum_{i \in I} P_i = \sum_{j \in J} P_j \leqslant KC$$
(7.2)

2. Attendance constraint

$$A_{pr} \geqslant a_{\min}$$
(7.3)

3. Do not get off until you reach your destination:

$$\sum A_{pr} = Q$$
(7.4)

4. Each site in rural areas can only be served once during operation:

$$\sum_{s \in S_0} \sum_{r \in p_s} \sum_{i \in I} \sum_{j \in I} x_{ijr}^s = 1$$
(7.5)

7.3 Algorithm design

7.3.1 Algorithm flowchart

The genetic algorithm is used to solve the rural demand-responsive bus route optimization model. The algorithm flowchart is shown in Figure 7.2.

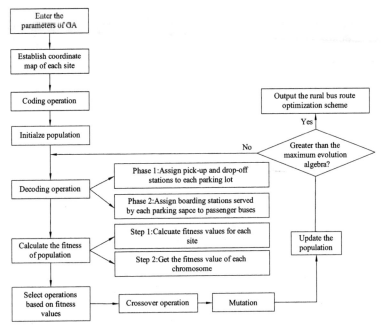

Fig.7.2　Algorithm flowchart

7.3.2　Coding and decoding design for passenger stations and other stations

Chromosomes are coded in decimal coding mode in this model, and the passenger stations in towns and the boarding stations or get-off stations in rural areas are numbered directly. The number of passenger stations is set as 0, and the numbers of boarding stations or get-off stations are 0, 1, 2, ..., n in turn.

7.3.3　Cross design

Provided the point crossing is used directly, some sites may be missed, therefore, the order crossing method is adopted. First, two hybridization points are randomly selected among parents, and then hybridization segments are exchanged, and other positions are determined according to the relative positions of parent sites. The crossover process is shown below.

Before crossing

0	3	2	5	| 7	8	1	9 |	6	4

Parent 1

2	9	5	3	| 4	7	6	8 |	0	1

Parent 2

Set the random hybridization points as 4 and 7. Then the chromosome of the offspring is:

&	&	&	&	| 4	7	6	8 |	&	&

Offspring 1

&	&	&	&	| 7	8	1	9 |	&	&

Offspring 2

Starting from the second cross section of parent 1 "6-4-0-3-2-5-7-8-1-9", we remove the elements in the cross section to get 0-3-2-5-1-9, and then fill in the chromosomes of the two offspring from the second hybridization point as follows.

After crossing

2	5	1	9	4	7	6	8	0	3

Offspring 1

3	4	6	0	7	8	1	9	2	5

Offspring 2

7.3.4 mutation operation

According to the given mutation rate, three integers within the interval are randomly selected for selected mutated individuals, such as $1<a<b<c<10$, and the gene segment between a and b is inserted after c and before 10.

7.4 Case study

The road network in Linxia City, Linxia Autonomous Prefecture, Gansu Province is taken as the research object, which is divided into two regions of the west and the east. The location of each station and passenger station is also marked in the following table and the following figure.

In the western road network, there is 1 passenger station in urban areas and 10 stations in rural areas. The nodes are shown in Table 7.2.

Tab. 7.2　Western road network node number, name and classification

Node number	Node name	Coordinate X/km	Coordinate Y/km	Classification
0	Suburban bus station	20	2.6	Passenger terminal (urban area)
1	Dalujia village	17	24	Get on/off station (rural area)
2	Chongtaiyuan village	9.7	23	
3	Jinggou village	4.2	17.5	
4	Yuwangzhuang	12.3	19.7	
5	Jiajiazui	10.3	14.5	
6	Songshuzhuang	14.7	13.5	
7	Gazhai village	12.2	9.3	
8	Shangshi village	8.1	6.22	
9	Chejiaping	4.1	2.5	
10	Hongshuihe	9.8	1.9	

Scatter map of coordinates in the western is shown in Figure 7.3.

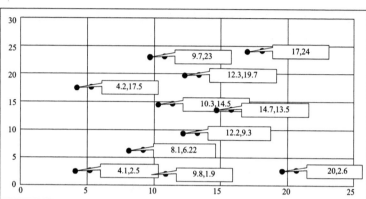

Fig.7.3   Scatter plot of coordinates of western rural stations and
passenger stations

In the eastern road network, there is 1 passenger station in the urban areas and 9 get on/off stations in the rural areas. Table 7.3 is node numbering.

Tab.7.3   Eastern road network node number, name and dassification

Node number	Node name	Coordinate X /km	Coordinate Y /km	Classification
0	South Bus Station of Linxia	2.1	22	Passenger terminal (urban area)
1	Zhangwangjia village	9.1	11.8	Get on/off station (rural area)
2	Xingshugou	10.2	4.1	
3	Zhaojiashan	14.1	3.9	
4	Bajia gou	19.5	1	
5	Sidou	16.2	10.1	
6	Gamajia	14.2	14.3	
7	Liujiashan	15.6	19.5	
8	Dingzhaojia village	22	22.3	
9	Dayangjia village	20.3	11.2	

The scatter plot of the site coordinates in the eastern region is shown in Figure 7.4.

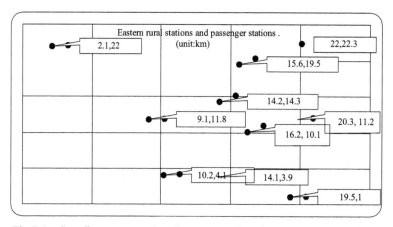

Fig.7.4　Coordinate scatter plot of eastern rural station and passenger station

According to the information of passengers who need to take the rural passenger bus collected by the mini program "Village-to-Village Passenger Transport", the number of passengers from Station 1 to Station 9 in the western region during the day is 3, 1, 7, 9, 10, 4, 4, 2, 12, 6 respectively; The number of people who need to return to each station in rural areas after departing from the passenger station in the western region at night is (the passengers who did not return to the station No.2 Chongtaiyuan Village and No.8 Shi Cun at night): 3, 7, 9, 10, 4, 4, 12 and 6.

The number of passengers who need to enter the city in the eastern region from station 1 to station 9 is 5, 9, 4, 7, 2, 10, 11, 8 and 3 respectively during the day. The number of people who need to return to each station in rural areas when departing from the passenger station in the eastern region at night is in order (there are no passengers who need to return to station No.5 for four fights at night): 5, 9, 4, 7, 9, 12, 7 and 4.

Use python to set the population size to 1000, the maximum evolutionary number to 200, the crossover probability to 0.8, and the mutation probability to 0.1. The length of the chromosome is determined by the total number of stations (on/off stations plus the number of passenger stations), and the nuclear load of passenger buses is 60 people/vehicle.

Set the diesel fuel cost per kilometer of the bus to 2 yuan, and the fixed cost of one operation is 30 yuan.

The solution result is shown in Fig.7.5-7.8.

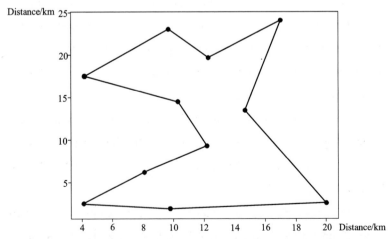

Fig.7.5　Daytime solution route map in the western region, bus number: 1

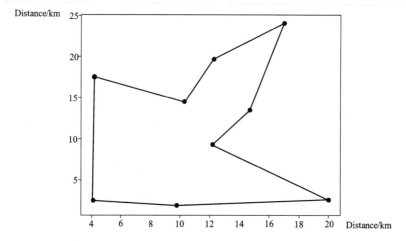

Fig.7.6　Solving route map in the western area at night, bus number: 2

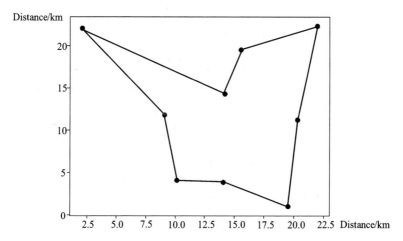

Fig.7.7　Daytime solution route map in the eastern region, bus number: 3

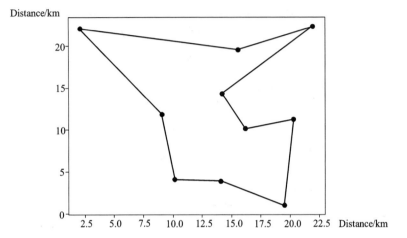

Fig.7.8   Route map for the eastern region at night, bus number: 4

The solution results are shown in Table 7.4. The results show that the model and algorithm can better complete the situation of rural demand-responsive public transportation.

Tab.7.4   Solution result

Serial number of buses	Serial number of Route sites	Running mileage/km	Bus operating cost/yuan
1 (Western daytime)	0-6-1-4-2-3-5-7-8-9-10-0	79.17	188.34
2 (Western night)	0-7-6-1-4-5-3-9-10-0	75.61	181.22
3 (Eastern daytime)	0-7-8-6-5-9-4-3-2-1-0	81.20	192.4
4 (Eastern night)	0-6-7-8-9-4-3-2-1-0	78.36	186.72
Total	-	314.34	748.68

7.5 Conclusions

(1) Aiming at remote and underdeveloped rural areas, we have changed the traditional route formulation similar to ordinary urban buses, installed rural demand-responsive buses, and developed the mini program "Village-to-Rural Passenger Transport" to collect passenger departure and arrival station demand, the route optimization is carried out under the above premise, and the buses are reasonably dispatched to get on & off passengers at the target stations, which not only meets the needs of passengers efficiently, but also reduces the cost of the bus company.

(2) This book uses decimal algorithm, special order crossing method and special mutation operation. The calculation based on the scatter diagram formed by the coordinates between each node. The on/off stations can only be served once, and the added demand constraints also improve the rationality of the ride, moreover, the resulting operating costs are also more ideal.

(3) In addition to the waste of resources caused by demand and supply in rural passenger transport, there are also major problems in terms of weak infrastructure and safety management. These aspects urgently require governments at all levels to increase policy support for rural passenger transport and rapid reform and development. Furthermore, the rapid development of electric vehicles can also make a great contribution to the cost control of buses in the future.

(4) The single objective model based on genetic algorithm is studied in this paper, and the driving speed and fuel consumption of

vehicles are set as fixed values. However, in the actual operation of rural passenger transport, in addition to the weather and climate, the influence of roads is relatively great, and the roads in some rural areas are rugged, which has an obvious impact on the actual driving speed of buses. Therefore, the driving speed and driving time can be set as an interval value in future research, of course, the problem will become more specific and more complicated, which requires the use of more complex models and more efficient algorithms.

7.6 Summary

At present, the operation efficiency of rural passenger transport is low, and most riding purposes of passengers cannot be achieved within a reasonable time period. In view of the unreasonable status quo that rural passenger transport is similar to the fixed line of ordinary urban bus transport. This chapter sets up a rural demand-responsive bus based on the collection of passenger demand information, and according to the problem description in the actual process, a route optimization model for rural buses with a single passenger station and multiple on/off stations on the basis of meeting passenger needs with the goal of minimizing the total operating cost is built. The passenger stations, boarding stations and getting off stations are numbered respectively through genetic algorithm, as well as the decimal mixed coding operation is used, the sequence crossover method and special design mutation operation are carried out. Taking a certain area in Linxia City, Linxia Hui Autonomous Prefecture, Gansu Province as an example, the east and west areas are set up. During the daytime, buses in urban passenger stations pick up passengers in rural areas and then return to the passenger stations, and at night, passengers in urban areas are sent back to various stations in rural areas in accordance with the demand, so as to verify the rationality of the model and algorithm. The results show that the genetic algorithm is of great significance to rural passenger transport because of its low cost and intuitive vehicle route.

7.7 References

[1] Lei Xing, Zhong Mei. The status quo and analysis of the development of rural passenger transport in Sichuan Province[J]. Transportation Energy Conservation and Environmental Protection, 2019, 15(3): 27-30.

[2] Lu Cunye. Research on the development model of rural passenger transport system under low-carbon economy[D]. Xi'an: Changan University, 2011.

[3] Hu Kunpeng. Research on the application of county-level rural passenger transportation planning methods[D]. Changsha: South China University of Technology, 2014.

[4] An Tong. Research on urban customized bus operation system and route design[D]. Changsha: Changsha University of Science and Technology, 2016.

[5] Zhang Fengyan, Zhou Wei. Research on rural highway passenger transport route optimization based on traffic compactness[J]. Highway and Transportation Science and Technology, 2010, 27(9): 111-116.

[6]   Zhang Minyi, Feng Si, Lyu Chenxi, Guo Lin. Customized bus route optimization model and solution algorithm[P]. Proceedings of the 9th China Intelligent Transportation Conference in 2014. China Intelligent Transportation Association: 2014, 1-8.

[7]   Qiu Guo. Research on optimization method of customized bus route design based on travel mode choice of passenger[D]. Beijing: Beijing Jiaotong University, 2019.

[8]   Shen Chan, Cui Hongjun. Research on optimization of real-time customized bus lines based on the shortest path reliability[J]. Transportation System Engineering and Information, 2019, 19(6): 99-104.

[9]   Zhang Hangqi. Research on customized bus route planning based on granular computing[D]. Hangzhou: Hangzhou Dianzi University, 2019.

[10]   Tao Lang, Ma Changxi, Zhu Changfeng, Wang Qingrong. Multi-objective optimization of customized bus routes based on genetic algorithm[J]. Journal of Lanzhou Jiaotong University, 2018, 37(2): 31-37.

[11]   Gao Yan. Research on the Route Planning of Village and Town Passenger Vehicles Concurrently Operating Express Delivery[D]. Beijing: Beijing Jiaotong University, 2020.

[12]   Cao Liufang. Optimization of urban and rural customized bus routes in rural areas with weak passenger flow[D]. Hefei: Hefei University of Technology, 2019.

[13]   Chen Xingying. Customized bus route generation and operation optimization under random user demand[D]. Xi'an: Chang'an University, 2019.

[14] Ma Changxi, Wang Chao, Hao Wei, Liu Jing, Zhang Zhaolei. Emergency customized bus line optimization under public health emergencies[J]. Journal of Traffic and Transportation Engineering, 2020, 20(3): 89-99.

[15] Xu Rongrong. Research on the Application of Demand-Responsive Public Transport in Rural Passenger Transport[D]. Xi'an: Chang'an University, 2015.

[16] Wang Jiao. Research on Customized Bus Stop Planning and Timetable Preparation[D]. Beijing: Beijing Jiaotong University, 2016.

[17] Wu Zhenyu. Urban customized bus network optimization for commuting needs[D]. Hefei: Hefei University of Technology, 2017.

Chapter 8

Robust optimization model and algorithm for demand-responsive rural passenger vehicles

8.1　Introduction

At present, China's economy and society are developing rapidly, and the urban transportation construction and development have achieved unprecedented achievements. Even the urban public transportation system is rapidly upgrading, the development of public transportation in vast rural areas is still slow and stagnant. In addition, although few rural areas have achieved the bus requirements of every village pass, the conflict between the low demand of passengers and the excessive supply of bus companies has caused a huge waste of resources. At peak times, the phenomenon that the limited number of fixed buses cannot pick up all passengers which, is common, so the demand-responsive buses in rural areas are emerged. The demand-responsive buses are a public transportation service mode between conventional buses and taxis. In the form of multiple people sharing transportation, it can meet the requirements of high-quality travel, although its price is slightly lower than that of common buses. High but also within a reasonable acceptable range. To realize the demand-responsive buses in rural areas, first collect passengers' departure and arrival station information through the "rural passenger transport village-to-village" program, and adjust the bus routes scientifically and reasonably to the greatest possible extent. Efforts to provide passengers with convenient services and save passengers' travel time. On the one hand, it improves the utilization rate of resources and ensures that meeting the needs of passengers. On the other hand, it also makes travel convenient and economical. Demand-responsive buses can ensure the basic ride service, i.e., of "one person, one person", reduce unnecessary wastes, save the cost of the bus company, and also set reasonable travel routes according to the needs of different customers. So for residents' travel in urban, and rural areas, it is an effective solution.

Nowadays, there are few researches on the optimization of demand-responsive bus routes in rural areas. But a lot of analysis and answers to rural passenger transport problems and research on route optimization of related customized buses/buses have been accumulated as follows.

Amirgholy et al.[1] used the analysis model to define the operating cost of the dynamic demand response bus system and the total generalized cost of user decision-making. Simulation analysis. Inturri et al. [2] proposed the basic model ABM for testing different service areas in the actual environment, and simulated the impact of path selection strategies on the overall performance of the system. Lin et al. [3] described the variable route bus dispatching model from the perspective of mixed integer programming, mainly considering the problems of bus operating costs and passenger travel expenses, establishing the model with the lowest system cost as the optimization goal, designing related algorithms, the model is solved and simulated to verify the validity of the model. Li [4] considered the current situation of the mismatch between urban development and public transportation development, summarized the operating principles, operating conditions and rules of the variable route bus system, and designed the variable route service area based on the actual national conditions of our country. The construction steps of, and learned from the traffic planning ideas, constructed the relevant target model to solve. Dou[5] regarded transfer convenience as a key factor for residents to choose public transportation travel mode, and built a timetable optimization model with the goal of minimizing the total transfer waiting time between lines within the research time range, and designed an approximate sample mean value Method to solve the algorithm. Guo [6] proposed the layout (based on factors such as the status and layout of rural township passenger stations, and by dividing the road network level within the layout area,) method of rural township passenger stations; finally, combined with quantitative and qualitative analysis, determined the layout needs of the layout area. The number of passenger stations in the country provides a reference for the layout of rural passenger stations. Zhang [7] started from the rural passenger transport in towns and villages, combined with the theory and practice of the existing passenger terminal facility configuration scale, and carried out a systematic study on the scale of township facilities. Through investigation and analysis of the existing basic conditions of my country's township passenger transport, combination of the actual situation, the empirical research is carried out with Jiangzhang Town as an example. Liu [8] took Chongqing rural passenger transport as the research object, considered the characteristics of rural residents' scattered living, non-concentrated travel patterns, and diversified demand, and expanded from the three aspects of rural passenger transport development status, operation mode and promotion methods. Research, using a combination of investigation and analysis and theoretical analysis, a functional model with the objective of minimizing the cost of rural passenger transport was established. Faroqi et al.[9] used GIS technology to optimize demand-responsive bus routes, and collected network data and commuting times in 6 areas of Tehran City, and finally evaluated and analyzed the analysis results.

Based on the above research results, the existing literature on demand-responsive vehicles in towns and rural areas is still required further improvement. First of all, some route optimization models for rural passenger transport only consider a single goal, but do not consider multiple goals. Secondly, most of them are just optimizing the path in a certain environment, and do not consider the operation of vehicles in an uncertain environment according to the actual road environment. Finally, according to the characteristics of rural passenger transport, there is no comprehensive consideration and distinction between passengers taking buses from the countryside to the bus terminal in the town during the day, and passengers returning to the rural areas from the bus terminal in the town at night. In view of the above concerns, this book starts from the actual situation, takes into account the characteristics of a rural passenger transport and two different scenarios of getting on and off during the day and night, and establishes rural demand response model with the minimum total travel time of passengers and the lowest cost of the passenger transport company as the optimization objective. The multi-objective robust optimization model of the passenger bus, and the improved NSGA-II algorithm is used to solve it to obtain a more robust route plan.

8.2 Robust modeling of demand-responsive passenger cars in urban and rural areas

8.2.1 Problem description

There are multiple pick-up and drop-off stations in rural areas, and multiple passenger stations in urban areas. Each station in the countryside can only be served by a customized bus during each operation, and it can only be served once. Each passenger bus has the same model, and the same load, and can serve multiple stations, but the passengers cannot exceed its normal load. The problem that needs to be solved is that, on the premise of meeting the passenger needs, we try to make the cost of the bus company and the total travel time of passengers minimize. The schematic diagram of the vehicle service path is shown in Figure 1. Among them, the rural demand- responsive bus service process is as follows: after the passengers enter their ride information into the small program "Rural Passenger Transport Village to Village", during the day, the bus departs from a certain passenger station according to the needs of the passengers, and goes to the pickup station in the rural pickup area to receive the passengers until it reaches the approved load. Quantity limit, after serving the last passenger who got off the bus, the bus returns to the passenger terminal of the original departure, and picks up all the customers who want to enter the city. At the same time, when customers staying in the city during the day and they want to go home at night, they also need to enter their ride information into the small program "Rural Passenger Transport Village to Village", and then arrive at the passenger station at the specified time and take the passenger bus. According to the prescribed route, the passengers will be sent back to the drop-off station to be reached, and finally returned to the original passenger station(Stations in rural areas are for passengers boarding during the day and for getting off at night).

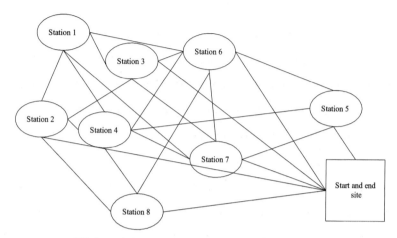

Fig.8.1　Schematic diagram of vehicle service route

8.2.2　Assumptions

According to the situation of transporting passengers in rural areas, some simplifications are made to the model, and the following assumptions are set:

1) The passenger station has the number of passenger cars that can meet the demand of all passengers in the road network, and each passenger car has the same model and the same approved capacity;

2) Each site can only be served once;

3) Each bus can serve multiple stations;

4) The number of passengers on and off stations has been determined, and the total number of passengers on each station will not exceed the approved capacity of a single passenger car;

5) The distance between different nodes is known;

6) Passengers do not get off the bus before arriving at the station that needs to be reached.

8.2.3 Symbol definition

Symbol definition is shown in Tab.8.1.

Tab.8.1 Symbol definition

Symbol	The meaning of the symbol or related factors	Type
S_0	A collection of demand sites in rural areas	set
S	Collection of passenger stations in urban areas, $S = \{s \mid s = 1, 2, \cdots, m\}$	set
d_{ijr}^s	The distance from the station i to the station j of the r-th bus at the s-th passenger terminal.	parameter
p_i	The number of people at the i-th getting on or off station	parameter
K	Operating passenger vehicles that carry passengers in the road network.	parameter
f	Fuel cost per kilometer for passenger cars	parameter
f_0	Other fixed costs per passenger car.	parameter
w	The collection of all sections in the passenger transport network.	set
d_{ij}	Distance of road section(i,j)	parameter
C	Number of authorized passengers per passenger car	parameter
Q_{pr}	The number of passengers on vehicle r on route p	parameter
V_s	$V_s = \{k \mid k = 1, 2, ..., k_m\}$ represents the collection of vehicles at the number.s passenger terminal, k_m represents the maximum number of vehicles.	set
x_{ijk}^s	$x_{ijk}^s = \begin{cases} 1, \textit{The } k-\textit{th passenger car at the } s- \\ \textit{th passenger terminal passes} \\ \textit{through the road section}(i, j) \\ 0, \textit{or} \end{cases}$	variable
Q	The total number of passengers who need to ride on the route	variable
D_{ijk}^s	The number of passengers on the k-th bus at the s-th passenger terminal when it travels from station i to station j	variable

Symbol	The meaning of the symbol or related factors	Type
I_{ijk}^s	$I_{ijk}^s = \begin{cases} 1, D_{ijk}^s > 0 \\ 0, D_{ijk}^s = 0 \end{cases}$	variable
R	A collection of road sections whose driving time has changed due to uncertain factors	set
Γ	Time Robust Control Parameters, $\Gamma \in [0, \mid w \mid]$	parameter
t_{ij}	The nominal value of the travel time of the passenger car on the road section, $t_{ij} = \dfrac{d_{ij}}{v}, (i,j) \in w$	parameter
$\hat{t}_{ij}$	The deviation of the nominal value of the travel time of the passenger car on the road section (i,j)	parameter
T_{ij}	$T_{ij} \in [t_{ij}, t_{ij} + \hat{t}_{ij}]$, Variable travel time of the passenger car on the road section (i,j) , $(i,j) \in w$	parameter
v	The speed of the passenger car, fixed value	parameter
E_i'	The number of passengers who have boarded the bus at the stop i and before the stop i	parameter

8.2.4 Model building

When constructing a route optimization model for rural or urban-rural areas, various factors need to be taken into consideration. The shortest vehicle path can not only meet the travel needs of passengers, but also reduce the operating costs of bus companies. At the same time, the road conditions in rural areas are different from those in cities, such as uneven or even rugged roads, too many curves, and vehicles. The poor infrastructure in the area will increase the driving time of vehicles and other difficulties, causing many problems for passengers. Therefore, setting the time required by the passenger car to an uncertain value is more suitable for reality. By optimizing the two goals of the lowest cost and the shortest passenger total travel time, one or more scientific and reasonable paths can be found, which reduces the number of bus companies. At the same time, we can try our best to satisfy the passengers, so that the passengers in the car can reach the destination faster.

Robust optimization is a kind of uncertain optimization, and it is also a kind of pre-analysis method, which has a wide range of applications in many fields. Robust optimization fully considers the uncertainty in the modeling process, and describes the variables in the form of sets. In 1973, Soyster used the idea of robust optimization to solve the uncertainty in linear programming for the first time. Although it was initially considered on the worst basis, the result was too conservative, it opened up the road of robust optimization. Mulvey et al. first proposed the concept of robust optimization in 1995 [10]. They gave a general model framework based on scenario set robust optimization, and proposed the concepts of solution robust and model robust, and eliminated the inconsistency by splitting the objective function into an aggregate function and a penalty function, and determined the influence of the parameters on the results. The Israeli scholars Ben-Tal and Nemirovski[11, 12] and the University of Berkeley's Ghaoui[13] put forward a foundational work on robustness in the 1990s. Ben-Tal proved that if the set U of uncertainty was an ellipsoid Uncertain sets, then for some of the most important general convex optimization problems (linear programming, quadratic constrained programming, semi-definite programming, etc.), the robust equivalence was either accurate or can be approximated as a solvable problem: Algorithms such as interior point method can be used to solve in polynomial time. In addition, Ben-Tal gave an approximate robust equivalence that can be handled in the calculation of general uncertain semi-definite programming problems. After that, Ben-Tal et al. put forward concepts such as adjustable robust optimization concepts, which were widely used in all walks of life. Later, Bertsimas and Sim [14] proposed a new robust optimization framework based on the research of Soyster, Ben-Tal and Nemirovski. The robust optimization of Bertsimas and Sim covered discrete optimization. The main feature was that the established robust equivalence did not increase the complexity of problem solving. On the other hand, the robust optimization of Bertsimas and Sim allowed the occurrence of constraint violation (Constraint Violation), in which case the robust solution obtained was feasible with high probability. The theories of Bertsimas and Sim had been widely recognized by the academic circles due to their ease of processing and practicality.

The robust optimization model of urban and rural demand responsive passenger transport is established as follows.

$$\min z_1 = \sum_{s \in S} \sum_{K \in \{V_s | s \in S\}} \sum_{(i,j) \in w} I_{ijk}^S X_{ijk}^S t_{ij} E_i' + \\ \max_{\{R / R \in w, |R| = \Gamma\}} \sum_{s \in S} \sum_{K \in \{V_s | s \in S\}} \sum_{(i,j) \in w} \hat{t}_{ij} I_{ijk}^S X_{ijk}^S E_i' \tag{8.1}$$

Since there is a "max" item in the objective function (8.1), the equivalent conversion of Bertsimas and Sim is required according to Bertsimas and Sim's robust optimization theory, and the resulting formula (8.2) looks like this:

$$z_1 = \Gamma \widehat{t_{IJ}} + \min[\sum_{s \in S} \sum_{K \in \{V_s | s \in S} \sum_{i=1:(i,j)}^{I:(I,j)} \sum_{j=1:(i,j)}^{J:(i,J)} t_{ij} I_{ijk}^s X_{ijh}^s E_i' +$$

$$\sum_{s \in S} \sum_{K \in \{V_s | s \in S} \sum_{i=1:(i,j)}^{I:(I,j)} \sum_{j=1:(i,j)}^{J:(i,J)} (\widehat{t_{ij}} - \widehat{t_{IJ}}) I_{ijk}^s X_{ijh}^s E_i'] \tag{8.2}$$

$$\min z_2 = f[\sum_{s \in S} \sum_{r \in p_s} \sum_{i \in S_0} \sum_{j \in S_0} d_{ijr}^S x_{ijr}^S +$$

$$\sum_{s \in S_0} \sum_{r \in p_s} \sum_{i \in S_0} \sum_{j \in S_0} d_{ijr}^S x_{ijr}^S + \sum_{s \in S_0} \sum_{r \in p_s} \sum_{i \in S_0} \sum_{j \in S} d_{ijr}^S x_{ijr}^S] + Rf_0 \tag{8.3}$$

s.t

$$\sum_{i \in s \in S_0} p_i \leqslant KC \tag{8.4}$$

$$\sum Q_{pr} = Q \tag{8.5}$$

$$\sum_{s \in S} \sum_{r \in p_s} \sum_{i \in S_0} \sum_{j \in S_0} x_{ijk}^s = 1 \tag{8.6}$$

In the above, x_{ijk}^s and I_{ijk}^s are 0-1 decision variables. The objective function of the type (1) and type (2) as the minimum total travel time of the passenger is the sum of the total time from each passenger to the arrival station after boarding the bus , and type (3) is the cost function of the bus company , which includes the fuel cost according to the length of the journey , as well as the fixed cost of the bus. Type (4) is a passenger capacity constraint; type (5) is a non-vehicle constraint when not at the destination; and type (6) indicates that each site in a rural area can only be serviced once during the operation of a vehicle. The Γ is the time-robust control parameters, which are used to control the degree of conservatism of the solution. Under different Γ values, the solution is different and the degree of conservatism is different.

8.3 Solve the algorithm

For a robust model with multiple objective functions, and cannot make two target functions at the same time achieve optimal, so multi-objective solution algorithm is used, unlike single-objective functions, there are conflicts between multiple objective functions, the optimization of one goal may cause the value of another goal worse, it is impossible to make multiple targets achieve optimal at the same time. Multi-target optimization results in a collection of non-poor solutions, the elements in the set are called Pareto optimal solutions. And the Pareto solution, also known as the non-dominant solution or non-dominance solution, is the best solution on one target and probably the worst on the other because of conflicts between goals and incomparable phenomena. These solutions, which are bound to weaken at least one other target function, are called non-dominant or Pareto solutions while improving any target function. The result of the solution is the need for a potentially large and widely distributed Pareto optimal solution. The fixed paper uses the improved NSGA-II fast non-dominant sorting algorithm to solve.

8.3.1 Simulates the adaptability function of the improved annealing thought

The idea of simulated annealing is used to stretch the adaptability with the number of iterations. Genetic algorithm in the early stage of operation of individual differences, if the use of roulette method to choose the generation and adaptability proportional, you can get a better selection effect, but in the later stage of the algorithm, the degree of adaptation tends to be consistent, the advantages of excellent individuals are insufficient, then the adaptability to a certain "stretch", the specific formula is as follows:

$$f_i = \frac{e^{f_i/T}}{\sum_{i=1}^{M} e^{f_i/T}} \tag{8.7}$$

$$T = T_0(0.99^{g-1}) \tag{8.8}$$

Where is the f_i i-th individual's fitness, M is population size, g is genetic algebra, T is temperature, T_0 is initial temperature.

8.3.2 Fast non-dominant sorting and crowding

8.3.2.1 Fast non-dominant sorting method

For each individual i, there are two parameters $n(i)$ and $S(i)$.

$n(i)$ is the number of solved individuals that dominate individual i in the population. $S(i)$ is a collection of dissolved individuals governed by individual i.

(1) First, find all the $n(i)$ and 0 individuals in the population and store them in the current collection $F(1)$.

(2) For each individual j in the current collection $F(1)$, examine the individual set $S(j)$ at its disposal and subtract n(k) of each individual k in set $S(j)$ by 1, i.e. the number of individuals that dominate individual k minus 1 (because the individual j that governs individual k has been deposited in the current set $F(1)$

(3) If $n(k)$-1-0 is deposited in another set of H. Finally, $F(1)$ is given as the first level of non-dominant individual collection, and given

the individual within the collection the same non-dominant order i(rank), and then continue to do the above classification of H and give the corresponding non-dominant order until all individuals are graded. The computational complexity is m as the number of target functions and N as the population $O(mN^2)$size

8.3.2.2   Determine congestion

1. Determine the degree of congestion

(1) The congestion degree i_d of each point is set to 0;

(2) For each optimization goal, the population is sorted non-dominantly, so that the crowding degree of the two individuals on the boundary is infinite. $o_d = l_d = \infty$;

(3) Calculate the crowding degree of other individuals in the population.

$$i_d = \sum_{j=1}^{m} (| f_j^{i+1} - f_j^{i-1} |) \tag{8.9}$$

2. Congestion degree comparison operator

After fast non-dominated sorting and crowding calculation, each individual i of the population has two attributes: Non-dominated order determined by non-dominated order $i(rank)$ and Crowdedness i_d.

When any one of the following two conditions is met, individual i can be selected to win.

Condition 1: $i(rank) < j(rank)$.

Condition 2: $i(rank) = j(rank)$ and $i_d > j_d$.

Condition 1 is used to ensure that the selected individual belongs to the superior non-inferior level in the population. Condition 2 is to select two individuals at the same dominance level based on the crowded distance, and the less crowded individual (that is, the more crowded) will be selected. According to these two selection conditions, the winning individual in the population is selected.

8.3.4 Algorithm flowchart

Improved NSGA-II algorithm flowchart is shown in Fig.8.2.

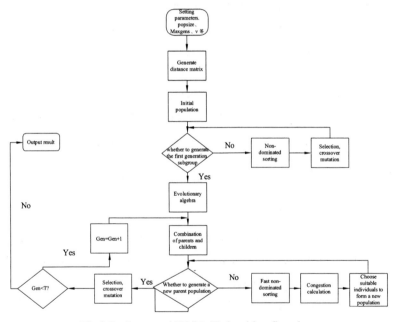

Fig.8.2　Improved NSGA-II algorithm flowchart

8.3.5 Algorithm steps

① Setting the specific values and other parameters of population size.

② After initializing the population, see if the first generation subgroup is generated, if it is generated, go to ③, if not, use non-dominated sorting and related selection cross-mutation operations to return to the beginning of ②.

③ Population evolution.

④ Combine the parent and offspring populations, and then see whether a new parent population is generated; if a new parent population cannot be generated, perform a fast non-dominated sorting method, through the crowding calculation, select suitable individuals to form a new population, and then judge whether to generate a new population Population; if a new parent population can be generated, proceed directly to the selection, crossover, and mutation operations to ⑤.

⑤ Determines whether the maximum number of iterations has been achieved and, if not, returns ④.

8.3.6 Coding and variation operation

8.3.6.1 Coding operation

The model encodes chromosomes by natural number coding and directly numbers passenger stations in towns and villages and stations in rural areas. Set the passenger station number to 0, the station or drop-off station number is 1, 2, ..., n.

8.3.6.2 Variation operation

According to the given mutation rate, the three integers within the interval are randomly taken for the individuals with the selected variation. For example: $1 < a < b < c < 10$, and insert the gene segment between a and b into the back of c and 10 front.

8.4　Case study

In this book, the road network of a district in Linxia City, Linxia Autonomous Prefecture, Gansu Province, was selected as the research object, and two different scenarios were set for day and night according to the actual situation of urban and rural passenger transport.

During the day, the bus departs from the city's passenger terminal empty, arrives at all the passenger demand points in the rural area to receive the passengers, the passengers do not get off the bus, and finally return to the departure of the city passenger terminal, all the passengers on board put down the bus.

At night, all passengers who need to return to the countryside board the bus at the city's passenger terminal, and the bus takes all passengers to the drop-off point in the rural area according to passenger demand and then returns to the city's passenger terminal.

The travel time of the section is $t_{ij} = \dfrac{d_{ij}}{v}$ nominally valued and the (i, j) deviation value of the vehicle's travel time on the section is $\hat{t}_{ij} (o \leqslant \hat{t}_{ij} \leqslant 0.5 t_{ij})$ randomly generated real number, Γ is a robust control parameter.

The fuel cost for each kilometer of bus driving is 1.5 yuan /km. The fixed cost for each bus is 30 yuan, and the passenger bus nuclear load is 50 people/bus.

Tab.8.2　site information

The node number	The name of the node	classify
0	Suburban bus station	Passenger terminal (urban area)
1	Dalujia village	
2	Chongtaiyuam village	
3	Jinggou village	
4	Yuwangzhuang	
5	Jiajia zui	
6	Sonashu zhuang	Get-on/off-bus stop (rural areas)
7	Gazhai village	
8	Shangshi village	
9	Chejiaping	
10	Houshi	
11	Songsishe	

Tab.8.3　Distance between sites　　　　in: km

Node	distance											
	0	1	2	3	4	5	6	7	8	9	10	11
0	0	4	5	6	4	5	4	5	2	3	9	6
1	4	0	4	6	2	3	7	3	4	5	2	10
2	5	4	0	6	5	4	4	3	7	2	8	9
3	6	6	6	0	8	5	4	3	5	4	6	2
4	4	2	5	8	0	4	4	5	6	7	3	5
5	5	3	4	5	4	0	5	4	3	5	7	3
6	4	7	4	4	4	5	0	5	9	6	4	2
7	5	3	3	3	5	4	5	0	6	4	9	5

Node	distance											
	0	1	2	3	4	5	6	7	8	9	10	11
8	2	4	7	5	6	3	9	6	0	2	4	7
9	3	5	2	4	7	5	6	4	2	0	6	5
10	9	2	8	6	3	7	4	9	4	6	0	8
11	6	10	9	2	5	3	2	5	7	5	8	0

Tab.8.3　Passenger information for each site

Site number	Number of passengers during the day	Number of unloading guests in the evening
0 (starting point)	0	0
1	5	4
2	3	2
3	2	5
4	3	5
5	7	10
6	6	6
7	4	4
8	6	6
9	2	2
10	3	3
11	2	2

Running the platform with visual studio code, the version of python is 3.8.3, solving using the improved NSGA-II algorithm, which sets the initial population at 120; the number of iterations at 120; the initial temperature in the simulated annealing fitness function: the $T_0 = 80$. Probability of variation is 0.3, and the cross probability is 0.6, the robust control parameters for setting the time are 0, 20, 40, and the results of running the program multiple times are shown in Tab.8.5 and 8.6, in the case of $\varGamma = 0$, 20, 40, 2, 3, and 3 sets of pareto optimal solutions are obtained respectively.

Tab.8.6　Program running results in daytime scene

$\varGamma$	Pareto solution	The vehicle travel path	Travel distance /km	Bus company cost/yuan	Total passenger travel time/min
0	1	0-4-10-1-5-7-3-11-6-2-9-8-0	33	79.5	438.15
	2	0-7-3-11-6-4-10-1-5-2-9-8-0	34	81	427.25
20	1	0-6-11-3-7-1-10-4-5-2-9-8-0	33	79.5	539.05
	2	0-7-3-11-6-4-10-1-5-2-9-8-0	34	81	516.86
	3	0-3-11-6-10-4-1-5-7-2-9-8-0	35	82.5	492.65
40	1	0-6-10-4-1-5-11-3-7-2-9-8-0	33	79.5	599.83
	2	0-3-11-6-4-10-1-5-7-2-9-8-0	35	82.5	598.35
	3	0-3-10-6-11-5-4-1-7-2-9-8-0	39	88.5	575.14

Tab.8.6　Program running results in the night scene

$\varGamma$	Pareto solution	The vehicle travel path	Travel distance /km	Bus company cost/yuan	Total passenger travel time/min
0	1	0-9-2-7-3-11-6-4-10-1-5-8-0	32	78	608.94
	2	0-8-9-2-7-3-11-6-4-10-1-5-0	33	79.5	589.53
20	1	0-8-5-1-10-4-6-11-3-7-2-9-0	32	78	655.67
	2	0-8-5-7-3-11-6-10-1-4-2-9-0	34	81	611.08
	3	0-8-5-1-7-3-11-6-10-4-2-9-0	35	82.5	603.11
40	1	0-9-2-7-3-11-6-10-1-4-5-8-0	32	78	725.81
	2	0-8-9-2-7-3-11-6-10-1-4-5-0	33	79.5	679.94
	3	0-8-9-2-7-3-11-6-4-1-5-10-0	41	91.5	675.17

The day and night solution results are shown in Fig.8.3 and 8.4.

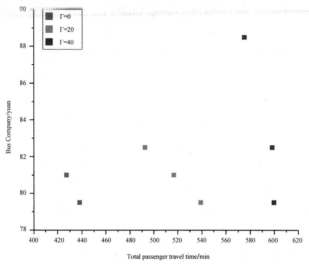

Fig.8.3　The pareto optimal solution at different Γ values during the day

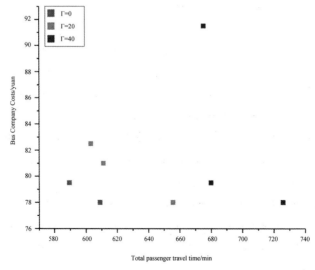

Fig.8.4　The pareto optimal solution at different Γ values at night

As you can see from Tab.8.5 and 8.6 of the results, Fig.8.3 and 8.4, the target values and different target values for each Pareto solution are obtained under different Γ values, and the shortest path is different. On the one hand, as the Γ value increases, the total passenger travel time target increases, and the minimum distance and cost target values change slightly. The model is also most sensitive to uncertain risks when the Γ is 0, and the optimal solution to the model may change when the weight of a section of the road driven by the bus changes. However, as the Γ grows, the model becomes more conservative, which is somewhat robust, and when the Γ is 40, the model is least sensitive to uncertain changes and the most conservative solution, resulting in relatively large passenger company costs and total passenger travel time. By looking at the changes in the solution, we can see that as the cost objective function value increases, the total passenger time target value decreases. And vice versa. This indicates a decrease in the distance travelled by buses, resulting in an increase in the total travel time of passengers. How to choose the optimal path in the specific problem, but also need to consider the influence of other factors to do specific analysis, through a large amount of data and according to the actual situation to make decisions.

When $\Gamma=0$, the improved NSGA-II algorithm used in this paper is compared with the traditional multi-objective genetic algorithm, and the results are shown in Table 6.

From the table comparison, it can be seen that the improved NSGA-II algorithm is superior to the traditional multi-target genetic algorithm, both day and night, when the Γ is 0. Compared with the traditional multi-target genetic algorithm, the improved NSGA-II has lower total passenger travel mileage and bus company cost during the day, 17.35% less passenger travel time, 56.52% lower program running time, and 54.17% lower total passenger travel time and 54.17% lower bus operating time than the latter. This shows that compared with the traditional multi-target genetic algorithm, the improved NSGA-II algorithm proposed in this paper is more ingenious, the results are better, and the task of urban and rural demand-based response bus can be better completed.

Tab.8.7   Algorithm comparison results

scenario	Compare metrics	Improve NSGA-II algorithm		Traditional multi-objective genetic algorithms	
		Pareto solution 1	Pareto solution 2	Pareto solution 1	Pareto solution 2
Day	Vehicle driving scheme	0-4-10-1-5-7-3-11-6-2-9-8-0	0-7-3-11-6-4-10-1-5-2-9-8-0	0-8-5-7-3-11-6-10-1-4-2-9-0	0-3-11-6-4-10-1-5-7-2-9-8-0
	Total operating mileage /km	33	34	34	35
	Passenger company cost / yuan	79.5	81	81	82.5
	Total passenger travel time /min	438.15	427.25	543.76	503.26
	Average passenger travel time /min	432.70		523.51	
	The operation time /s	10		23	

续表

scenario	Compare metrics	Improve NSGA-II algorithm		Traditional multi-objective genetic algorithms	
		Pareto solution 1	Pareto solution 2	Pareto solution 1	Pareto solution 2
Night	Vehicle driving scheme	0-9-2-7-3-11-6-4-10-1-5-8-0	0-8-9-2-7-3-11-6-4-10-1-5-0	0-8-9-2-7-3-11-6-10-1-4-5-0	0-7-3-11-6-4-10-1-5-2-9-8-0
	Total operating mileage /km	32	33	33	34
	Passenger company cost / yuan	78	79.5	79.5	81
	Total passenger travel time /min	608.94	589.53	723.46	632.47
	Average passenger travel time/min	599.235		677.965	
	The operation time /s	11		24	

8.5 Conclusions

(1) As a relatively backward urban and rural areas, the development of passenger transport system is not yet mature, and responsive passenger buses provide efficient and convenient services for those with clear destinations by collecting the needs of all owners, meeting the needs they could not meet in the past. This is a great waste

of resources for solving the actual situation that the operating environment in rural areas is not good, the contradiction between the low demand for passengers and the oversupply of bus companies has caused a huge waste of resources, and the number of fixed buses for mass travel during peak periods cannot carry all passengers. The phenomenon, a better and more complete solution is given.At the same time, taking into account the actual situation of urban and rural passenger operation, passengers travelling behaviors during the day travelling from the countryside to the town's passenger terminal and at night returning from the town's passenger terminal to rural areas, are different.

(2) This book fully takes into account the uncertainty of the running time of vehicles on the road caused by such factors as uneven and rough roads, and aims at minimizing the cost of bus companies and minimizing the total travel time of passengers. a robust optimization model of urban and rural responsive passenger transportation is established. To obtain an optimal solution of the model, the improved NSGA-II algorithm is developed ensuring the shortest possible total passenger travel time when the cost of the bus company is as small as possible. This not only brings economic benefits to the bus company, but also considers the impact of travel time for passengers. This is also more valuable than considering only single-objective functions or line optimization in a defined environment.

(3) Comparing the improved NSGA-II algorithm proposed in this book with the traditional multi-target genetic algorithm. During the day, the total mileage of bus operations and bus company costs are lower

than the latter, the total passenger travel time is saved 17.35%, the program running time is saved 56.52%, in the evening, the total mileage of bus operations and bus company costs are lower than the latter, passenger travel time is saved 11.61%, the program running time is saved 54.17%. This shows that the improved NSGA-II algorithm designed in this paper is superior to the traditional multi-target genetic algorithm and more valuable, whether it is the solution result or the solution efficiency.

8.6 References

[1] Amirgholy M, Gonzales E J. Demand responsive transit systems with time-dependent demand: User equilibrium, system optimum, and management strategy[J]. Transportation Research Part B, 2016, 92: 234-252.

[2] Inturri G, Giuffrida N, Ignaccolo M. Testing demand responsive shared transport services via agent-based simulations[J].New Trends in Emerging Complex Real Life Problems, 2018(12): 313-320.

[3] Lin Yeqian, Li Wenquan, Qiu Feng. An Optimal Model for Flex-route Transit Scheduling Problem[J]. Journal of Transport Information and Safety, 2012, 30 (5): 14-18

[4] Li Zheng. Research on service area design for flexible transit system[D].Nanjing: Southeast university, 2017.

[5] Dou Xueping. Research on coordinated scheduling of integrated public transport system[D]. Nanjing: Southeast university, 2016.

[6] Guo Wenwen. Study on the layout of rural township passenger station [D]. Xi'an: Chang'an University, 2012.

[7] Zhang Ruiqin. Study on construction scale of the township passenger station based on the rural public passenger transportation[D]. Xi'an: Chang'an University, 2013

[8] Liu Liangping. Chongqing rural passenger transport operation mode and method research[D]. Chongqing: Chongqing Jiaotong University 2014.

[9] Faroqi H, Sadeghiniaraki A. Developing gis-based demand-responsive transit system in Tehran city[J]. International Conference on Sensors & Models in Remote Sensing & Photogrammetry, Kish Island, Iran, 2015, 189-191.

[10] Mulvey, J. M., Vanderbei, R. J. and Zenios, S. A. Robust optimization of large-scale systems[J]. Operations Research, 1995(43): 264-281.

[11] Ben-Tal, A. and A. Nemirovski, Robust convex optimization[J]. Mathematics of Operations Research, 1998. 23(4): 769-805.

[12] Ben-Tal, A. and A. Nemirovski, Robust solutions of uncertain linear programs[J]. Operations Research Letters, 1999, 25(1): 1-13.

[13] ElGhaoui L, Lebret H. Robust solutions to least-squares problems with uncertain data[J]. SIAM Journal on matrix analysis and applications, 1997.18(4): 1035-64.

[14] Bertsimas, D. and M. Sim, The price of robustness[J]. Operations Research, 2004, 52(1): 35-53.

Appendix

The main source codes for chapter 6

```cpp
#include<algorithm>
#include <cmath>
#include <iostream>
#include <time.h>
#include<stdlib.h>
#include<float.h>
using namespace std;

#define PopSize 100
#define MaxGens 100
#define N 27
#define K 13
#define PC 0.8
#define PM 0.1
```

```
#define C 20
#define t 0.0084 //(h)
#define V 20//(km/h)


int city[N];
int begin_city=0;


double    r[28][28]={

    {0,0,0,0,0,0,0,0,0,0,0,0,0,0,0,0,0,0,0,0,0,0,0,0,0,0,0,0},//0
    {0,0,5,6.3,7.6,12,11,10,13,6,15,14,17,8,7,13,11,9,8,16,11,14,10,7,
4.5,8.8,5.5,7.8},//a
    {0,5,0,4.8,5.6,4.8,6.9,5.5,6.9,8.8,7.8,5.8,6.9,7.5,8.9,5.7,15,8.9,7.8,
9.9,7.6,6.8,5.8,6.9,7.8,6.8,8.5,7.8},//1
    {0,6.3,4.8,0,8,12,15,13,7,6,23,12,7,9,11,12,10,11,6,8,15,11,10,8,1
1,13,8,6},//2
    {0,7.6,5.6,8,0,5.6,6.9,7.1,8,10,12,8.9,7.7,6.6,8.9,8.2,6.9,5.7,14,10,
8,7,9,11,8.9,7.9,8.9,5.4},//3
    {0,12,4.8,12,5.6,0,10,11,9,7,5,6,7,9,10,11,8,5,8,9,14,13,12,11,16,1
0,14,11},//4
    {0,11,6.9,15,6.9,10,0,10,6,7,8,8,9,10,15,7,6,10,18,11,6,7,8,9,14,6,
8,15},//5
    {0,10,5.5,13,7.1,11,10,0,5,4,3,8,6,16,11,12,17,10,9,8,7,6,12,10,9,8
,7,6},//6
```

{0,13,6.9,7,8,9,6,5,0,9,7,8,6,7,8,6,7,9,8,11,10,6,7,8,13,13,15,9},//
7

{0,6,8.8,6,10,7,7,4,9,0,14,16,10,8,9,6,11,8,10,8,9,10,8,8,9,10,14,1
0},//8

{0,15,7.8,23,12,5,8,3,7,14,0,9,8,10,8,9,8,7,9,7,9,8,6,7,9,11,14,13},
//9

{0,14,5.8,12,8.9,6,8,8,8,16,9,0,11,9,7,9,8,10,14,9,10,14,9,8,8,7,9,
14},//10

{0,17,6.9,7,7.7,7,9,6,6,10,8,11,0,2,5,4,6,7,9,10,8,9,14,8,9,10,9,15}
,//11

{0,8,7.5,9,6.6,9,10,16,7,8,10,9,2,0,9,8,7,6,7,9,12,6,8,10,6,5,8,9},//
12

{0,7,8.9,11,8.9,10,15,11,8,9,8,7,5,9,0,5,6,7,9,8,4,6,7,8,10,6,9,10},/
/13

{0,13,5.7,12,8.2,11,7,12,6,6,9,9,4,8,5,0,8,9,16,7,9,6,12,6,8,9,13,6}
,//14

{0,11,15,10,6.9,8,6,17,7,11,8,8,6,7,6,8,0,6,9,10,9,8,13,8,9,10,11,8
},//15

{0,9,8.9,11,5.7,5,10,10,9,8,7,10,7,6,7,9,6,0,9,10,8,7,6,8,5,9,7,10},
//16

{0,8,7.8,6,14,8,18,9,8,10,9,14,9,7,9,16,9,9,0,9,10,9,7,6,8,9,10,14}
,//17

{0,16,9.9,8,10,9,11,8,11,8,7,9,10,9,8,7,10,10,9,0,6,9,7,8,6,10,9,12
},//18

{0,11,7.6,15,8,14,6,7,10,9,9,10,8,12,4,9,9,8,10,6,0,12,6,9,7,9,10,4
},//19

```
{0,14,6.8,11,7,13,7,6,6,10,8,14,9,6,6,6,8,7,9,9,12,0,9,10,6,10,9,14
},//20
    {0,10,5.8,10,9,12,8,12,7,8,6,9,14,8,7,12,13,6,7,7,6,9,0,9,11,9,8,7},
//21
    {0,7,6.9,8,11,11,9,10,8,8,7,8,8,10,8,6,8,8,6,8,9,10,9,0,9,8,12,14},/
/22
    {0,4.5,7.8,11,8.9,16,14,9,13,9,9,8,9,6,10,8,9,5,8,6,7,6,11,9,0,8,7,9
},//23
    {0,8.8,6.8,13,7.9,10,6,8,13,10,11,7,10,5,6,9,10,9,9,10,9,10,9,8,8,0
,9,10},//24
    {0,5.5,8.5,8,6.8,14,8,7,15,14,14,9,9,8,9,13,11,7,10,9,10,9,8,12,7,9
,0,8},//25
    {0,7.8,7.8,6,5.4,11,15,6,9,10,13,14,15,9,10,6,8,10,14,12,4,14,7,14
,9,10,8,0},//26

    } ;

int people_number[14]={0,10,8,13,18,16,7,14,20,9,12,20,6,13};

double p[28][28]={

    {0,0,0,0,0,0,0,0,0,0,0,0,0,0,0,0,0,0,0,0,0,0,0,0,0,0,0,0},//0
    {0,0,0,0,0,0,0,0,0,0,0,0,0,0,0,0,0,0,0,0,0,0,0,0,0,0,0,0},//a
    {0,0,0,0,0,0,0,0,0,0,0,0,0,0,0,0,0,0,0,0,0,1,0,0,0,0,0,0},//1
    {0,0,0,0,0,0,0,0,0,0,0,0,0,0,0,0,1,0,0,0,0,0,0,0,0,0,0,0},//2
    {0,0,0,0,0,0,0,0,0,0,0,0,0,0,0,0,0,0,0,0,0,0,0,0,0,0,1,0},//3
```

```
{0,0,0,0,0,0,0,0,0,0,0,0,0,0,0,0,1,0,0,0,0,0,0,0,0,0,0,0},//4
{0,0,0,0,0,0,0,0,0,0,0,0,0,0,0,0,0,0,0,0,1,0,0,0,0,0,0,0},//5
{0,0,0,0,0,0,0,0,0,0,0,0,0,0,0,0,0,0,0,0,0,1,0,0,0,0,0,0},//6
{0,0,0,0,0,0,0,0,0,0,0,0,0,0,0,0,0,0,0,0,0,0,0,1,0,0},//7
{0,0,0,0,0,0,0,0,0,0,0,0,0,0,0,0,0,0,0,0,0,0,0,1,0,0,0},//8
{0,0,0,0,0,0,0,0,0,0,0,0,0,0,0,0,0,0,0,0,0,0,0,0,0,0,0,1},//9
{0,0,0,0,0,0,0,0,0,0,0,0,0,0,0,0,0,1,0,0,0,0,0,0,0,0,0,0},//10
{0,0,0,0,0,0,0,0,0,0,0,0,0,0,0,0,0,0,0,1,0,0,0,0,0,0,0,0},//11
{0,0,0,0,0,0,0,0,0,0,0,0,0,0,0,0,0,0,0,0,0,0,1,0,0,0,0},//12
{0,0,0,0,0,0,0,0,0,0,0,0,0,0,0,0,0,1,0,0,0,0,0,0,0,0,0,0},//13
{0,0,0,0,0,0,0,0,0,0,0,0,0,0,0,0,0,0,0,0,0,0,0,0,0,0,0,0},//14
{0,0,0,0,0,0,0,0,0,0,0,0,0,0,0,0,0,0,0,0,0,0,0,0,0,0,0,0},//15
{0,0,0,0,0,0,0,0,0,0,0,0,0,0,0,0,0,0,0,0,0,0,0,0,0,0,0,0},//16
{0,0,0,0,0,0,0,0,0,0,0,0,0,0,0,0,0,0,0,0,0,0,0,0,0,0,0,0},//17
{0,0,0,0,0,0,0,0,0,0,0,0,0,0,0,0,0,0,0,0,0,0,0,0,0,0,0,0},//18
{0,0,0,0,0,0,0,0,0,0,0,0,0,0,0,0,0,0,0,0,0,0,0,0,0,0,0,0},//19
{0,0,0,0,0,0,0,0,0,0,0,0,0,0,0,0,0,0,0,0,0,0,0,0,0,0,0,0},//20
{0,0,0,0,0,0,0,0,0,0,0,0,0,0,0,0,0,0,0,0,0,0,0,0,0,0,0,0},//21
{0,0,0,0,0,0,0,0,0,0,0,0,0,0,0,0,0,0,0,0,0,0,0,0,0,0,0,0},//22
{0,0,0,0,0,0,0,0,0,0,0,0,0,0,0,0,0,0,0,0,0,0,0,0,0,0,0,0},//23
{0,0,0,0,0,0,0,0,0,0,0,0,0,0,0,0,0,0,0,0,0,0,0,0,0,0,0,0},//24
{0,0,0,0,0,0,0,0,0,0,0,0,0,0,0,0,0,0,0,0,0,0,0,0,0,0,0,0},//25
{0,0,0,0,0,0,0,0,0,0,0,0,0,0,0,0,0,0,0,0,0,0,0,0,0,0,0,0},//26

};
```

```
int generation;
int CurBest;

struct GenoType
{
    int gene[N];
    double fitness;
    double fitnessl[K];
    double rfitness;
    double cfitness;

};

  typedef struct
{

int vehiclePos[13][13];

}VP;
VP vp[PopSize];

struct ResultType
{
    double best_val;
    double avg;
    double stddev;
```

```
};

GenoType population[PopSize+1];
GenoType newpopulation[PopSize+1];
ResultType result[MaxGens];
void initialize();
void InitializeVehicle();
void AssignVehicles();
void evaluate();
void Find_the_best();
void elitist();
void select();
void crossover();
void mutate();
void report();
int IntGenerate();

void swap(int *,int *);

void swap(int *a,int *b)
{
    int temp;
    temp=*a;
    *a=*b;
    *b=temp;
}
```

```
int IntGenerate1()
{

int a=1,b=13;
int rand1=(rand()%(b-a+1))+a;
return rand1;
}

int IntGenerate2()
{

int a=14,b=26;
int rand2=(rand()%(b-a+1))+a;
return rand2;
}

void initialize()
{
        int matrix1[N],matrix2[N];
        int begin_city=0;
        int x1,x2,i,j;

        for( i=1; i<=13; i++)
            matrix1[i]=i;
```

```
for(j=0;j<PopSize;j++)
{
        population[j].gene[0]=begin_city;

    for( i=0;i<13;i++)
    {
        x1=0; x2=0;
        while(x1==0)
        x1=IntGenerate1();
        while(x2==0)
        x2=IntGenerate1();
        swap(&matrix1[x1],&matrix1[x2]);
    }
        for(int i=1;i<=13;i++)
            population[j].gene[i]=matrix1[i];

}

for( i=14;i<=26;i++)
matrix2[i]=i;
for( j=0;j<PopSize;j++)
{
for(i=14;i<=26;i++)
{
    x1=0;x2=0;
    while(x1==0)
```

```
                x1=IntGenerate2();
            while(x2==0)
                x2=IntGenerate2();
                swap(&matrix2[x1],&matrix2[x2]);
    }
    for(int i=14;i<=26;i++)
        population[j].gene[i]=matrix2[i];
    }


void InitializeVehicle()
{
    for(int j=0;j<PopSize;j++)
for(int i=0;i<13;i++)
        for(int k=0;k<13;k++)
            vp[j].vehiclePos[i][k]=0;
}
void evaluate()
{
    int begin_city = 1;
    int next_city,current_city;
    int k=0,s=0;
    int i,j,ii=0,jj,z=0;

    for(j=0;j<PopSize;j++)
    {
    for(k=0;k<13;k++)
```

```
            {
                population[j].fitnessl[k]=0;
            }
        }

    for(j=0;j<PopSize;j++)
    {

    for(k=0;k<13;k++)
    {
                s=0;ii=0;z=0;
                int b[14]={0};
                int a[14]={0};
                int s1 = 0;
                if(vp[j].vehiclePos[k][s] == 0)
                {
                    break;
                }
                current_city = begin_city;

                for(s=0;s<13;s++)
                {

                        if(vp[j].vehiclePos[k][s] == 0)
                    {
                            break;
```

```
                    }

          next_city = vp[j].vehiclePos[k][s];

          population[j].fitnessl[k] += 2*t*people_ number
[next_city];

          if(current_city != begin_city)
          {

          population[j].fitnessl[k] += ((r[current_city]
[next_city+1])*people_number[s1])/V;

          }

          if(0 <= s)
          {
          people_number[s1]   +=   people_number[vp[j].
vehiclePos[k][s]];

          }

          current_city = next_city + 1;

       for(jj=14;jj<=26;jj++)
```

```
            {
                if(p[current_city][jj+1]!=0)
                {
                        a[ii]=jj;
                        ii++;
                }
            }
        }

    for(z = 0; z < 14; z++)
        {
            if(b[z]!=0)
            {
                    next_city = population[j].gene[b[z]];

                    population[j].fitnessl[k]  += ((r[current_city]
[next_city+1])*people_number[s1])/V;

                    current_city = next_city + 1;

                    for(int m1 = 1; m1 <= 13; m1++)
                        {
if(p[m1+1][current_city] != 0)
                                {
                                                 people_number[s1]
```

```
= people_number[s1] - people_number[m1];

                                              }
                                    }
                              }
                          }

              }

          population[j].fitness=0;

          for(k=0;k<13;k++)
          {
                  population[j].fitness += population[j].fitnessl[k];
          }
      }
  }

  {
      int mem,i;
      CurBest=0;
      for(mem=1;mem<PopSize;mem++)
      if(population[mem].fitness<population[CurBest].fitness)
      CurBest=mem;

      for(i=0;i<N;i++)
```

```
        population[PopSize].gene[i]=population[CurBest].gene[i];
        population[PopSize].fitness=population[CurBest].fitness;
}

void elitist()
{
 int i;
 double best,worst;
 int best_mem,worst_mem;
 best=population[0].fitness;
 worst=population[0].fitness;
 best_mem
 for(i=0;i<PopSize-1;++i)
 {
        if(population[i].fitness<population[i+1].fitness)
        {

                if(population[i].fitness<=best)
            {

                        best=population[i].fitness;
                        best_mem=i;
            }

                if(population[i+1].fitness>=worst)
            {
```

```
                worst=population[i+1].fitness;
                worst_mem=i+1;

        }
    }

    else
    {
            if(population[i].fitness>=worst)
            {

                    worst=population[i].fitness;
                    worst_mem=i;
            }

            if(population[i+1].fitness<=best)
            {

                    best=population[i+1].fitness;
                    best_mem=i+1;
            }
    }

}
if(best<=population[PopSize].fitness)
    {
```

```
        for(i=0;i<N;i++)

population[PopSize].gene[i]=population[best_mem].gene[i];

population[PopSize].fitness=population[best_mem].fitness;
    }
    else
    {
        for(i=0;i<N;i++)

population[worst_mem].gene[i]=population[PopSize].gene[i];

population[worst_mem].fitness=population[PopSize].fitness;
    }
}

void select()
{
    int mem,i,j;
    double sum=0.0;
    double p;
    double x[PopSize];

    for(mem=0;mem<PopSize;mem++)
        sum+=population[mem].fitness;
    for(mem=0;mem<PopSize;mem++)
```

```
        x[mem]=sum-population[mem].fitness;
    sum=0.0;

    for(mem=0;mem<PopSize;mem++)
        sum+=x[mem];

    for(mem=0;mem<PopSize;mem++)
        population[mem].rfitness=x[mem]/sum;

    population[0].cfitness=population[0].rfitness;

    for(mem=1;mem<PopSize;mem++)
    {
        population[mem].cfitness=population[mem-1].cfitness+population
[mem].rfitness;
    }

    for(i=0;i<PopSize;i++)
    {
    p=rand()%1000/1000.0;
    if(p<population[0].cfitness)
        newpopulation[i]=population[0];
    else
    {
        for(j=0;j<PopSize;j++)
        if(p>=population[j].cfitness && p<population[j+1].cfitness)
```

```
          newpopulation[i]=population[j+1];
     }
   }

for(i=0;i<PopSize;i++)
   population[i]=newpopulation[i];
}

void crossover()
{
   int i,j;
   int min,max,flag;
   double x;
   for(i=0;i<PopSize;i++)
      {
   x=rand()%1000/1000.0;
   if(x<PC)
   {
     min=0;
     max=0;
     while(min==0)
       min=IntGenerate1();
     while(max==0)
       max=IntGenerate1();
     if(max<min)
      {
```

```
    int temp;
    temp=max;
    max=min;
    min=temp;
    }
    flag=max;
    for(j=min;j<=(max+min)/2;j++)
    {
    swap(&population[i].gene[j],&population[i].gene[flag]);
    flag=flag-1;
    }
  }
    }
    for(i=0;i<PopSize;i++)
    {
x=rand()%1000/1000.0;
if(x<PC)
min=0;
max=0;
  while(min==0)
    min=IntGenerate2();
    while(max==0)
    max=IntGenerate2();
if(max<min)
    {
    int temp;
```

```
        temp=max;
        max=min;
        min=temp;
        }
        flag=max;
        for(j=min;j<=(max+min)/2;j++)
        {
        swap(&population[i].gene[j],&population[i].gene[flag]);
        flag=flag-1;
        }
        }
}

void mutate()
{
 int i;
 double x;
 int x1,x2;

 for(i=0;i<PopSize;i++)
 {
        x=(int)rand()%1000/1000.0;
        if(x<PM)
        {
            x1=0;
            x2=0;
```

```
            while(x1==0)
            x1=IntGenerate1();
            while(x2==0)
            x2=IntGenerate1();
            swap(&population[i].gene[x1],&population[i].gene[x2]);
        }
    }

for(i=0;i<PopSize;i++)
{
        x=(int)rand()%1000/1000.0;
        if(x<PM)
        {
            x1=0;
            x2=0;
            while(x1==0)
            x1=IntGenerate2();
            while(x2==0)
            x2=IntGenerate2();
            swap(&population[i].gene[x1],&population[i].gene[x2]);
        }
}
}

void report()
{
```

```
int i;
double best_val;
double avg;
double stddev;
double sum_square;
double square_sum;
double sum;

sum=0.0;
sum_square=0.0;

for( i=0;i<PopSize;i++)
{

  sum+=population[i].fitness;
  sum_square+=population[i].fitness*population[i].fitness;
}
avg=sum*1.0/(1.0*PopSize);
square_sum=avg*avg*PopSize;
stddev=sqrt((sum_square-square_sum)/(PopSize-1));
best_val=population[PopSize].fitness;

result[generation-1].best_val = best_val;
result[generation-1].avg = avg;
result[generation-1].stddev = stddev;
}
```